T0386298

SAMBAL SHIOK

MANDY YIN

THE MALAYSIAN COOKBOOK

Photography by Louise Hagger

Hardie Grant

QUADRILLE

CONTENTS

INTRODUCTION

MY MISSION IN LIFE IS TO INTRODUCE AS MANY PEOPLE AS POSSIBLE TO MALAYSIAN CUISINE.

The food of Malaysia is a result of the unique merger over centuries of indigenous Malay ingredients and cooking methods with external influences, adapting ingredients and techniques from countries such as China, India, Portugal, Spain, the Netherlands and even Britain. Many dishes delicately balance sweetness, sourness and saltiness, often marrying chilli heat and a hint of bitterness.

In this book, my aim is to highlight a cross-section of Malaysian cooking: Malay, Indian, Chinese, Peranakan and tribal Iban. Much like the food I cook at my London restaurant, Sambal Shiok Laksa Bar, I want to celebrate the diversity of the country and its people. This book showcases a selection of Malaysian-inspired recipes from snacks, pickles and salads, to noodle soups, rice dishes, curries and sweet delights. The recipes include many family stalwarts together with those that I have developed for the restaurant. They can be used for weekday family meals, dinner parties or celebrations. Malaysians love to celebrate any occasion and we don't need much of an excuse for a feast! At a family get-together, we like sharing food and it is perfectly normal to see a huge variety of stir fries, curries and stews served with as much rice as you can manage; snacks; fried noodles contrasted with refreshing salads; pickles, chilli dips and sauces, all served at once. Malaysian dishes are food for the soul and offer full-on, in-your-face, satisfying flavours.

These recipes are true to me, my experiences and my food memories. Several of my dishes are not what you may traditionally find in Malaysia but are firmly rooted in Malaysian flavours. All cuisine has evolved over decades and centuries. I like to think I'm doing my forefathers

and foremothers proud – my ancestors from China who moved over to Malaysia and started doing their thing with the local ingredients and cuisine, generally mixing things up!

Typically, Malaysian meals showcase a variety of spicy, fried, braised, steamed and boiled meat and vegetables. Delicious and healthy fresh vegetables and a great variety of herbs are used to create colourful salads and mouth-watering dishes. Not all Malaysian dishes are chilli-hot but if you are looking to cook and enjoy spicy Malaysian dishes, you will find this cookbook useful. Once you have collected the basics of a Malaysian larder like shrimp paste, lemongrass, tamarind and coconut milk, anyone can cook a multitude of intricately layered Malaysian dishes in a home kitchen with ease.

There are fewer than a handful of specialist ingredients needed, with most of those used at the restaurant available in regular supermarkets. Only a small number of the recipes (such as laksa or prawn noodle soup) involve longer ingredient lists or are more time-consuming – these would interest the more intrepid cook or someone who likes a challenge. I do not add artificial monosodium glutamate as a seasoning in any of my dishes (other than the small amounts already present in store-bought oyster sauce or chilli oil), as I believe Malaysian food is flavourful enough without its use.

You will find that the vast majority of the recipes are easy or, at most, require intermediate cooking skills. Some recipes may appear intimidating at first because of their relatively long list of ingredients, but the method will really be quite simple. Many dishes revolve around a *rempah* spice paste being blitzed up before simply being stir-fried or braised within a sauce. The *rempah* is where the magic happens

– the combination of ingredients within it and then frying it off with patience to allow its components to sing.

In this book, there are plenty of options for vegetarians and vegans, as well as those observing halal, dairy-free and/or gluten-free diets. Where necessary, I adapt my food to cater for these requirements, for example, where a recipe traditionally calls for shrimp paste, dried shrimp or pork, I have made an effort in my restaurant to adapt and develop recipes to remove those elements, coming up with vegetarian or vegan versions that are just as tasty. In my Signature Curry Laksa (page 70) I have replaced shrimp paste with miso and tomato pastes, which results in a rich, tangy vegan broth instead.

Since starting my journey into the food industry in 2013, I have fed thousands and turned so many on to the possibilities and intricacies of Malaysian flavours.

Spicy, pungent, no-holds-barred flavours are my calling card. Having the restaurant has given me a voice to tell my story. Yes, we specialize in my Signature Curry Laksa (page 70) and Assam Laksa (page 74) both from a Peranakan Nyonya roster of recipes, but it has also given me the chance to shine a light on lesser-known dishes from Malaysia and to explore different regions or underexposed culinary cultures of the country.

My goal in life is to draw attention to the fact that Malaysian food is accessible and crying out for people to explore its variety. My greatest hope is that this book will inspire you to try cooking Malaysian food, to seek it out and eat it wherever you live and, ultimately, to travel to Malaysia to fully understand and experience the richness of its cuisine and culture.

For fellow Malaysians, I hope that you will find great comfort in these pages, as I did recreating nostalgic tastes while testing recipes and writing this book during the lockdowns of 2020's coronavirus pandemic.

WHAT IS SAMBAL?

Is it a pickle? Is it a condiment? A dipping sauce? It is all of them and more. Importantly, it is that special little *je ne sais quoi* that Malaysian cooks offer on the side of every meal, to add chilli heat for additional oomph to whatever dishes are on the table. Sambals are often made by home cooks in a large quantity and then stored for several weeks in the fridge in an airtight container.

Sambal variations are endless. In the case of an accompaniment to a laksa, sambals are quite commonly served in a small saucer on the side of the bowl or in a spoon perched on top of the noodles along with calamansi lime. Some people may like to stir the whole lot into the soup and noodles but the trick is to dab a little on each spoonful of noodles before it gets to your mouth! At the restaurant, however, as my signature laksa is already fiery by default, no sambal is served on the side.

WHAT IS SHIOK?

Shiok in Malay slang means a thing or an experience that is 'shockingly good'.

So, *sambal shiok* means 'shockingly good sambal'!

MANDY YIN

ORIGINS OF MALAYSIA'S FOOD CULTURE

Malaysian food has an incredible variety as a result of the country being a melting pot of peoples and cultures, both past and present.

To understand Malaysian food, you have to understand how the country is made up. It consists largely of three races: Malays (60 per cent), Chinese (25 per cent) and Southern Indians (7 per cent), with the 8 per cent balance made up of many tribal indigenous peoples. Imagine the array of flavours and influences from just these four cultures. Then there are also influences from neighbouring Thailand and Indonesia. Malaysian cuisine is a fusion of all these cultures, where each culture has taken interesting features from the others and applied it to their own cuisine.

As a side note, I would say that I am of Malaysian nationality but I do not call myself Malay. Similarly, it is incorrect to refer to all Malaysian food as Malay, as I shall now explain.

Malays use lemongrass, chillies, onions, garlic and ginger to make incredibly fragrant spice pastes as the base of most of their dishes. They also often use *empat sekawan* (four friends) – cinnamon sticks, cardamom, star anise and cloves – to infuse soups and stews. These give the dishes an unmistakeable warmth and depth.

Chinese tradesmen started coming to Malaysia in the 1400s. Many settled to work and live in Malaysia and brought with them their love of noodles, which explains the wide variety of fantastic noodle dishes all across the country. They come in soups, fried, braised in claypots and are made from rice, wheat, mung bean, sweet potato and so on. The Chinese also brought with them dishes like Hainanese chicken rice, from the island of Hainan, just south of China, which the Malays then adopted as their own, adding spice to the chicken and

grilling it instead of poaching it. A dish like *bak kut teh* (Pork Herbal Soup on page 86) was Chinese in origin, but when it reached Malaysian shores, the cook made use of the superb peppercorns available from Sarawak to enhance its flavours and added lethal fresh-cut bird's eye chillies in soy sauce as a condiment to suit the local palate.

South Indians migrated to Malaysia for work in the last two centuries and brought with them a panoply of flavours and dishes. *Roti canai*, a flaky flatbread served with a vegetable, fish or meat-based curry, has become a ubiquitous all-day snack. The curries served with it are firmly embedded in every Malaysian's taste memory – soothing, mild lentil, comforting chicken, rich mutton and fish sour with tamarind. Indians also share with the Malays their love of charcoal-grilling fresh seafood, and once in Malaysia, started to use banana and pandan leaves to accentuate and add flavour to their cooking.

Malaysia, of course, also has a colonial past and some dishes have elements of Eurasian cooking, for example the use of tomato ketchup in fried rice or sauces like *ayam masak merah* (red cooked chicken) or Worcestershire sauce in oxtail stews. Eurasians are typically people of any mixed-European and Asian ancestry. The Eurasians in Malaysia are also known as Kristang, and their cooking deserves a book in its own right.

Peranakan or **Nyonya** culture comes from the Peranakans and these two words are used interchangeably when talking about the cuisine. Peranakans are descendants of early Chinese traders who settled in Malaysia (Malacca first, and then later Penang), Thailand, Singapore and Indonesia. The Chinese men who settled in the region started marrying local Malay women and this created a special group of people who hold both Chinese and Malay cultural aspects and values. Instead of communicating in a Chinese dialect, they usually speak a patois of Malay and English. The old Malay word *Nyonya*, a term of respect and affection for Peranakan women of prominent social standing (part 'madame', part 'auntie'), has come to refer to the cuisine of the Peranakans. The word *Baba* denotes a Peranakan man.

Nyonya cooking is the result of blending Chinese ingredients with various spices and cooking techniques used by the Malay, Indonesian and Thai communities. This gives rise to Peranakan interpretations of dishes from these respective cuisines that are both tangy, aromatic, spicy and herbal. In other instances, the Peranakans have adopted Malay cuisine as their own and adapted it to their own palate. Some such dishes are *ikan assam pedas*, a spicy fish curry made sour from tamarind, and *rendang*, a spiced, slow-cooked stew with makrut lime leaves. Key ingredients include coconut milk, galangal/ginger, laksa leaf (also known as *polygonatum odoratum* or *daun kesum* in Malay, and hot mint or *rao ram* in Vietnamese), pandan leaves, *belacan* (fermented shrimp paste), tamarind, lemongrass, torch ginger flower (a vibrant pink flower with a unique sharp, almost citrusy yet floral fragrance) and makrut lime leaf.

There are regional variations in Nyonya cooking. Dishes from the island of Penang in the northern part of Peninsular Malaysia possess Thai influences, such as the more liberal use of chillies, tamarind and other sour ingredients. Dishes from Singapore and Malacca show a greater Indonesian influence, such as the use of coconut milk. The Peranakan in general

have quite a sweet tooth and so there are some savoury dishes that can veer towards the sweeter side.

I am continuing this fusion of influences by mixing Malaysian flavours with ingredients, dishes or techniques more readily available in the UK, or drawing on inspiration from my travels across Europe and America. My starting point when cooking is mainly Peranakan, but it is also heavily influenced by Chinese, Mamak (Tamil/South Indian), Malay, Thai and Indonesian cuisine.

MEMORIES OF MALAYSIA

I am Malaysian-born Chinese with Peranakan Nyonya heritage, born in Kuala Lumpur. Both of my grandmothers were from Penang, my maternal grandfather was from Hainan in the South China Sea, and my father and his father were true-blue Peranakan Baba, hailing from Malacca. The windows at the front of my restaurant have the words Malaysia, Kuala Lumpur, Penang and Malacca painted in gold for this reason.

I am thankful for having known all four of my grandparents as a child. Some of my strongest memories are of family feasts at their houses, especially around Chinese New Year, where each of my grandmothers would have spent days cooking around 20 different dishes, including snacks and sweet treats, for the whole family to enjoy over the festive period. There would also be frequent and lavish family banquets to celebrate birthdays or weddings.

My favourite banquets would be at large seafood restaurants, with live fish, crabs or lobsters swimming in big tanks – the fattest and best would be chosen by my father or uncles to be transformed into a mind-boggling array of dishes. Black pepper crab, lobster noodles with ginger and spring onions, whole steamed fish with shiitake mushrooms, soy sauce and sesame. Other memorable banquets would be held at large Chinese restaurants where there would be at least ten courses usually starting with roast suckling pig or shark fin soup (before changing societal values deemed this unacceptable), and ending with delicious *woh peng* (crispy, brown, red-bean pancakes), a special treat eaten at celebratory meals like Chinese New Year and wedding banquets. Red is a lucky colour so red bean paste, used in the pancake fillings, bring good luck! I have never found these pancakes on the menus of any Chinese restaurant in London – perhaps they are something one needs to pre-order from a secret menu? I also now know how to make shark fin soup without the shark fin, and so have included this recipe as it can be made simply or more elaborately as you wish.

I ate everything I was given as a child because everything I was given was so good! My parents instilled in me an openness to try anything once and if I didn't like it, that was fine. It also helped that everyone around me simply loved food and that all conversations seemed to come back to what the next meal was going to be, where the best noodles could be found or what new great eatery or stall my aunt/uncle had discovered that week. My mum craved and ate laksa frequently while she was pregnant with me. So, it makes sense that for as long as I can remember, I've eaten chillies and have had a high tolerance and enjoyment of them.

My mum was a housewife for most of my early childhood and she would have dinner ready for us all to sit down and eat, like clockwork, at 6 p.m. when my dad would return from work. When I was in primary school, tuition was a regular occurrence after dinner. After tuition we would hit the night markets to buy snacks for *siu yeh* (supper) at around 8.30 p.m., which was always something I looked forward to.

At the weekends, my father, who loved driving, would take us on jaunts to the seaside to places like Port Dickson or Port Klang where we would feast on butter prawns and grilled fish with sambal, among other wonderful dishes. It is also totally normal to Malaysians to drive a fair distance, following a tip from a family friend about a great place to eat somewhere out in the sticks. We are always willing to travel for good

food. I have fond memories of family holidays up to Ipoh where we would stuff ourselves silly with *kway teow th'ng* (fishball noodle soup) and also to Terengganu where we were introduced to *nasi kampung* (Malay economy rice), where a choice of at least 30 different dishes would be on offer and the chosen dishes were then ladled generously over piles of steaming white rice.

My brother and I used to go to Sunday school while my parents attended the service at the Methodist church next to the Federal Highway in Petaling Jaya, a suburb of Kuala Lumpur. I have fond memories of Sundays, not because of this church-going experience, but because of the lunches we would be treated to afterwards! These lunches would range from large trays of dumplings and various snacks of dim sum, *yong tau fu* (fish-paste stuffed vegetables) and slippery *chee cheung fun* (rice noodles), *lor bak* (a fantastic variety of deep-fried morsels wrapped in beancurd skin and dipped in chilli sauce) or my favourites, Indian *roti canai* (crispy, flaky flatbreads) and *thosai* (thin crispy crêpes – sometimes served impressively tall, standing on a plate like a witch's hat) served with chutneys or condensed milk.

The availability of anything you could possibly want to eat at any time of day is truly astounding, and is largely down to a 'can-do' mentality of Malaysians. The entrepreneurial spark of a hawker being able to conduct business practically anywhere, going hand-in-hand with the consumer's willingness to overlook rough and ready, slapdash surroundings while they are eating.

This gives rise to the prevalence of street food across the country – *pasar malam* (night markets) where hawkers set up stalls on roadsides with cars and motorcycles happily whizzing past; hawker centres and *kopi tiam* (coffee shops) with foldaway tables and plastic stools spilling out onto the adjoining walkways or roads. Many vendors, especially in more rural areas, simply set up a long wooden table to display their wares outside their front door or at the end of their road. Some just attach nifty apparatus to their bicycle or motorbike

and drive to their chosen sales patch where it unfolds into a makeshift stall. Most eateries, markets and hawker centres will have a roof but their sides will be open-air, with fans whirring on the ceilings to cool their customers.

I moved to London with my family when I was eleven years old, and so I am blessed with these vivid memories of the vibrant food culture of Malaysia.

Thankfully, it wasn't too much of a culture shock when my parents moved us all to London as I was already fluent in English. In Malaysian state schools during my childhood, Malay was the main language, so all lessons were taught in Malay except, of course, English. However, my father had always spoken English at home even as a child and his Malay was excellent (as is usual for Peranakan families), whereas my mother spoke Cantonese/Hainanese with her parents and English with her siblings and my brother and I. So, both my parents would speak English to me while I was growing up as this was their common tongue.

The biggest difference when we moved to London was the food culture. I quickly learnt that food wasn't as important to the British as it was back home. For example, a typical secondary school lunch for me would be tomato cup-a-soup from a vending machine, along with chicken nuggets and chips. I have always detested pizza, probably due to the terrible ones served at the school canteen. I do not remember anything freshly cooked or green. This was in stark contrast to the lunches I remember from primary school in Malaysia where the school canteen resembled a small food court, with different aunties hawking their wares. You could choose from *nasi lemak* – rice served with a vast array of dishes, including both vegetables and meat – laksa, chicken rice. So much choice! Curry laksa used to be my lunch of choice every day at primary school, so it is no surprise that my restaurant specializes in laksa!

Moving to London meant the end of breakfast, brunch and lunch at hawker stalls and coffee shops serving noodle soups or *roti canai*, no more night markets with the endless array of snacks and street food, no more Nyonya *kueh* cakes. Breakfast became toast with jam or a bowl of cereal. I was incredibly lucky that my mum is an amazing cook and remained a housewife until my late teens. This meant that at least our dinners would still be firmly rooted in our heritage. Many of the recipes in this book come from the dishes my mum used to make while I was growing up and that she still makes to this day.

MY KITCHEN AND USING THIS BOOK

Malaysian food lends itself to a huge variety of dishes, which can all be made at home and adapted according to different tastes. In my recipes, I include ideas for ingredient substitutions, like ways to make a dish vegan or vegetarian. I LOVE a good chilli kick so never deseed them, but if you prefer to use less chilli powder than a recipe calls for, the end result will still be incredibly tasty. Similarly, don't be put off if you don't have one or two of the seasoning or spice paste ingredients – generally the end result will still be great. This is the beauty of Malaysian cooking, especially when making smaller batches at home. You can tinker with the recipes to make them your own!

Wherever you see 'finely chopped', using a food processor to do so is absolutely fine. You can of course do it by hand if you so wish, but my preference is always to use a food processor or blender for finely chopping any more than a couple of garlic gloves! Similarly, I am not precious about using a pestle and mortar to pound spice pastes (my mum has used a food processor my whole life to create fantastically tasty food). More laborious methods were fine a hundred years ago when women were more or less confined to the kitchen and housework. Peranakan recipes especially represent an element of one-upmanship, with Nyonya ladies trying to outdo each other with ever more elaborate dishes and an ingredient list longer than her neighbours'! Women in that society had the time and were expected to create all these amazing dishes pounded by hand. Peranakan recipes were usually family secrets and passed down the generations. Nothing was written down in the old days but nowadays, recipes are easily available. There is nothing wrong with using a food processor to blitz your laksa spice paste or anything else. Time is money, as they say – or happiness, in my book.

Many of my recipes will call for a spice paste blitzed into a fine purée. I have found that the best way of achieving this at home is to use a handheld stick blender with a tall-sided container or bowl for smaller amounts, or a blender for larger quantities. Using a food processor or a blender for smaller amounts will generally not give you a fine enough paste.

When a spice paste includes lemongrass, you will need to roughly chop the stalks up into smaller pieces before blitzing it into a paste. If any sauce looks a bit lumpy after being cooked, blitz it with a handheld stick blender until it's a fine consistency. I do this often as I do not have a strong blender at home! Just remember to blitz the sauce before you add any substantial proteins, or alternatively take out the proteins from the sauce temporarily before blitzing it with the stick blender, as suits the particular recipe. The only thing that I would use a pestle and mortar for is the Sambal Belacan (page 108) and also to grind spices like peppercorns in the absence of a spice grinder.

Malaysians often use the term *pecah minyak*, meaning 'when the oil separates' to know when a spice paste has been fried off for long enough – and when it has been, you'll see the oil separating from the paste. When the oil seeps out of a spice paste containing chillies, it will be an attractive deep red.

◇◇◇◇◇◇◇◇◇◇◇◇◇◇◇◇◇◇◇◇◇◇◇◇◇◇◇◇◇◇◇◇◇◇

To make a dish vegan or vegetarian, I would make the following substitutions:

- Swap oyster sauce for mushroom or vegetarian stir-fry sauce.
- Rather than dried shrimp, shrimp paste or dried anchovies, use miso paste, tomato paste, salt or soaking water from rehydrating Japanese konbu dried seaweed sheets.

◇◇◇◇◇◇◇◇◇◇◇◇◇◇◇◇◇◇◇◇◇◇◇◇◇◇◇◇◇◇◇◇◇◇

Small, round Asian shallots are traditionally used in Malaysian cooking, as that is what is common locally. I have simply used white onions which are found everywhere in the UK. There is no great difference between shallots and white onions, or at least nothing that can't be fixed with a little extra sugar and/or frying off. The only recipe that calls for the sweeter Asian shallots are Fried Shallots (page 23) as they have a lower water content and so turn out crispier and sweeter than white or red onions.

◇◇◇◇◇◇◇◇◇◇◇◇◇◇◇◇◇◇◇◇◇◇◇◇◇◇◇◇◇◇◇◇◇◇

I often freeze fresh chillies. I wash them, dry them, take off the tops and then straight into freezer bags they go. They come out a bit soft and wet once defrosted but are totally fine to cook with. If you want to finely slice them for garnish or to add to a bit of soy sauce as a condiment, simply slice them with a sharp chef's knife when still frozen.

◇◇◇◇◇◇◇◇◇◇◇◇◇◇◇◇◇◇◇◇◇◇◇◇◇◇◇◇◇◇◇◇◇◇

Both metric and imperial measurements (plus US cups) appear within these recipes, but it is important to work with just one set of measurements and not to alternate between the two within a recipe. It is assumed that all aromatics like onions, ginger and garlic, and vegetables like carrots, potatoes etc., will be peeled before use. When using lemongrass in a spice paste, remove the end and any hard outer leaves first.

◇◇◇◇◇◇◇◇◇◇◇◇◇◇◇◇◇◇◇◇◇◇◇◇◇◇◇◇◇◇◇◇◇◇

Generally, I have avoided using coconut palm sugar in as many dishes as possible in this book, as I find that dark brown sugar gives pretty much the same effect in terms of final colour and sweetness. Palm sugar is widely (and cheaply) available in Southeast Asia, so if you are based there, of course please use it for all of these recipes. The only recipes I would strongly recommend hunting down good-quality palm sugar for (ideally from Malacca and very dark brown in colour due to careful caramelization) are the sweets in this book.

◇◇◇◇◇◇◇◇◇◇◇◇◇◇◇◇◇◇◇◇◇◇◇◇◇◇◇◇◇◇◇◇◇◇

I have simply stated 'white sugar' for a few recipes where I do not want the colour of the sugar to affect the end result. You can use granulated or caster (superfine) sugar here. Where it is a soup, you can use Chinese rock sugar if you have it available. As always, I have just tried to make the recipes as easy and as accessible as possible.

◇◇◇◇◇◇◇◇◇◇◇◇◇◇◇◇◇◇◇◇◇◇◇◇◇◇◇◇◇◇◇◇◇◇◇◇◇

I am not really too fussy about what noodles I use. For example, in Malaysia, you will find a whole host of different noodles served with laksa depending on which hawker stall you go to or which town or region you are in: egg noodles, rice vermicelli, *kway teow/ho fun* flat rice noodles and thicker, bouncier Assam laksa noodles. In Singapore, you will find thicker, round rice noodles. I love dried noodles in all their forms as they are so versatile, and also fresh *ho fun* noodles if you can find them. The main thing to note about dried noodles is that if you want to stir-fry them, you have to take care not to overcook them in the first instance. If using rice vermicelli, just soak them in cold water until they are pliable. Do not cook or soak them in boiling water as they will be too soft and just turn to mush when you try to fry them. For thicker dried noodles, rinse or plunge into cold water immediately as soon as they are cooked through to stop them cooking further. For noodle soups, cook any dried noodles according to the instructions on the packet before rinsing thoroughly under cold water in a colander to get rid of excess starch – this prevents them sticking together.

◇◇◇◇◇◇◇◇◇◇◇◇◇◇◇◇◇◇◇◇◇◇◇◇◇◇◇◇◇◇◇◇◇◇◇◇◇

After deep-frying, I will usually keep the frying oil to be used a couple more times as it seems a great shame to waste it. I let the oil cool in the pan before straining it, using a fine sieve (strainer), into a container. Alternatively, if you need to use the pan immediately afterwards, decant the hot oil carefully into a heatproof container to cool. Just note that any oil which has already come into contact with fish or seafood should only be used to fry fish or seafood in the future as it will have taken on a fishy smell. I tend to only discard used oil when it has turned more of a caramel colour.

◇◇◇◇◇◇◇◇◇◇◇◇◇◇◇◇◇◇◇◇◇◇◇◇◇◇◇◇◇◇◇◇◇◇◇◇◇

STORE-CUPBOARD STAPLES

Most of the ingredients called for in this book can be found at any good East Asian supermarket or online. Generally, they will last for months in your pantry or fridge. Remember that these recipes are a guide, so feel free to chop and change a few ingredients here and there. Savoury dishes are especially forgiving if you are missing one or two ingredients. Having a larder well-stocked with a few basic Asian sauces and spice powders does of course go a long way, and I have listed my store cupboard essentials and utensils below. I have tried as much as possible to give my preferred brand of store-bought products to help you recreate what we do at the restaurant.

Bean paste
This is a Chinese fermented soybean paste. Fu Chi is my preferred brand – I usually pick up the chilli version which is just ever so slightly spicy.

Black vinegar
This adds a unique tartness to sauces, soups and stir fries. It's also good for dressing dumplings. I like the Chinkiang brand.

Chilli flakes (red pepper flakes)/dried chillies
Generally, if a recipe calls for dried chillies, it will be the dried, long Chinese chillies you will find in East Asian supermarkets. However, I have found that chilli flakes are an easy substitute – one tablespoon of rehydrated dried chilli flakes is the equivalent of five whole dried chillies. Dried chillies are used to give dishes a rich red colour.

Chilli oil
I like the Lao Gan Ma range of chilli oils, popular all over the world. In particular I tend to buy the chilli crisp.

Chilli sauces and sambals
The most popular chilli sauce in Malaysia is Lingham's. It is widely used diluted with a bit of lime juice (or water) for all sorts of deep-fried snacks and steamed dumplings. The lime juice cuts through and lifts its sweetness. Simply add juice from one lime to a whole bottle of Lingham's if diluting in bulk. Otherwise just pour out whatever quantity of Lingham's you need into a small serving bowl before squeezing in and stirring through a bit of lime juice.

I don't tend to use shop-bought versions of sambal *oelek* a lot as I make my own – Simple Chilli Sauce (page 34). Also known as *chilli bol*, it is very useful for a pure chilli hit as sambal *tumis* tends to be sweeter.

I generally always have some Sambal Tumis (page 46) hanging around in my fridge – because it has been cooked off, it lasts for a long time and is handy to chuck into other dishes for a chilli hit.

Fresh chillies in soy
This is a widely used condiment that will add oomph to noodle and rice dishes which aren't already chilli-centric, particularly the Chicken and Garlic Noodle Soup (page 60), Charred Rice Noodles in Egg Gravy (page 64), Hainanese Five-spice Pork Chops (page 116), Anchovy Fried Rice (page 54), as well as Pork Herbal Soup (page 86).

To make a batch enough for up to three people, finely slice four fresh red or green chillies (you can also add a couple of finely sliced bird's eye chillies if you want an extra kick) and mix with 100ml (scant ½ cup) light soy sauce.

Coconut milk

We have historically used Chaokoh at the restaurant. I also like Aroy-D as it has a high coconut milk content and is good value for money. Kraw-Thip is very good for Malaysian desserts or sweet soups as it has the highest coconut milk content. Avoid any brands which use thickeners. Just after opening a can of coconut milk, be sure to give its contents a stir to fully incorporate any thicker coconut cream that has settled on top of the more liquid milk below.

Cornflour (cornstarch)

This is used frequently as a thickener for sauces and as a binding agent for minced meat or fish.

Curry leaves

Any mention of these throughout the book refers to fresh curry leaves. Fresh curry leaves can be picked from their stalks and then frozen indefinitely for later use. Dried curry leaves do not have enough flavour nor fragrance and have a dusty texture so are best avoided.

Fried curry leaves

Heat 100ml (scant ½ cup) oil in a small frying pan over a medium heat. Fry a handful of fresh curry leaves for 10 seconds, then place them on a paper towel to drain any excess oil. Fried curry leaves will keep for months in an airtight container and can be added as a quick garnish to many things. You can drizzle the curry leaf oil on curries like the Mamak Indian Lentil Curry (page 143) or use it as a base for stir fries.

Curry powder

My favourite brand of Malaysian curry powder is Adabi. Curries made using any of its varieties (meat, fish or seafood) are truly a taste of home for me. Make an effort to source a Malaysian curry powder wherever you are in the world, even if it is online, as it'll give you an incredible depth of flavour.

Garlic oil and confit garlic

Garlic oil is the star of the Chicken and Garlic Noodle Soup (page 60) and is a useful base for simple vegetable stir fries. Finely slice each clove from 3 whole bulbs of garlic. Fry in 200ml (scant 1 cup) of oil until light golden brown.

You can use the resulting confit garlic slices in your stir fries, or even better, mashed up with some salt and spread on toast. Instant garlic bread!

Garlic powder

This is really useful for adding to vegetable stir fries when you are out of fresh garlic or short of time. It's also useful for dry marinade powders and dough.

Laksa leaves (hot mint)

Its Malay name is *daun kesum*. You will usually find these in Vietnamese supermarkets as it is a popular herb in Vietnam, where it's called *rau ram*. There is no real replacement for laksa leaf – plain mint can be substituted but its fragrance doesn't have the same citrus hit as the laksa leaf.

Makrut lime leaves

You will find these frozen at most East Asian supermarkets. If being included in a spice paste, the stalks should be removed as they are very tough. If you are just using the leaves for infusing in a sauce, you can leave the stalks on.

Avoid dried lime leaves for the same reasons as dried curry leaves!

Oil

A neutral oil (such as vegetable, peanut or sunflower oil) must be used for all the recipes in this book. Do not use olive oil as its flavour is too strong and incompatible with these dishes.

Oyster sauce

My favourite brand is Lee Kum Kee Premium Oyster Sauce. It's the brand my mother has always used because it has the highest oyster content. As a vegan substitute I use Mushroom Stir Fry Sauce, also from Lee Kum Kee.

Pandan leaves

Fresh pandan leaves are a wild grass found everywhere in Malaysia and are affectionately known as the Southeast Asian vanilla.

I would not generally recommend using pandan essence, as the fragrance is nonexistent and I dislike the weird fluorescent green it produces in the end product. Freshly made pandan essence is 100 per cent worth the effort. All you need are fresh pandan leaves, blitzed with a bit of water in a blender or using a handheld stick blender, then strained through a piece of muslin (cheesecloth) to extract its truly heavenly smell and a beautiful grass-like greenness.

Peanuts

I usually use peanuts that have already been skinned. When a recipe calls for dry-toasting peanuts (or other nuts or seeds), simply toast them in a small frying pan without oil over a medium–low heat, stirring every now and then, until the nutty aroma is released and the peanuts start to brown a little.

Rice

I am a white rice disciple as it is the best at soaking up tasty sauces. At home I tend to use shorter grain white rice – Thai jasmine or premium double water polished long grain. I am not that fussy about particular brands of rice, the main thing being to cook it properly until fluffy. The only type I wholeheartedly reject is Uncle Ben's as it remains hard and pellet-like even after cooking, and doesn't absorb sauces at all.

White rice vinegar

The brand I use is Amoy.

Salt

All recipes simply use table salt.

Sesame oil

My favourite brand is Yeo's Pure Sesame Oil. Always make sure to buy the pure good stuff, never blended. Never use sesame oil to cook or stir-fry as it has a very low smoking point.

Its beauty is in its delicate fragrance which comes to the fore best when added straight before serving a dish. Generally speaking, use it as you would extra-virgin olive oil, as a finishing touch.

Fried shallots and shallot oil

Where a recipe calls for fried shallots, store-bought will be fine, though if you have the time, please do fry your own – it will be worth it as home-fried shallots are 100 per cent more fragrant than store-bought.

Crispy sweet shallots work really well with dishes like my Black Pepper Lamb Soup (page 90), Chicken and Garlic Noodle Soup (page 60) and Hainanese Chicken Rice (page 50). They are also delicious to give a final flourish to any stir-fried vegetables and congee.

The bonus is that you will end up with a good amount of residual shallot oil – liquid gold that will impart a beautiful fragrance to stir fries or fried rice when you use it as the base oil (and it'll save you having to chop up any onions). Big win!

When I fry shallots, I always make a massive batch as they keep well in an airtight container (any will do but preferably not plastic) kept in a cool, dry place for a few weeks.

1. Finely slice 250g (9oz) small, round Asian shallots.

2. Heat 350ml (1½ cups) oil in a medium saucepan over medium heat. The oil is hot enough when a quick, steady stream of bubbles rise around a single wooden chopstick when held upright in the oil.

3. Fry the shallots in two batches until light brown. They will continue cooking in the residual heat so be sure to remove them from the oil as soon as they reach this colour.

4. Drain the fried shallots on a fresh paper towel to soak up any excess oil ensuring they crisp up.

5. Once the shallot oil has cooled, it keeps well at room temperature for a month.

Shaoxing rice wine

Used in many Chinese dishes. A splash in a stir fry or marinade for meat or fish before stir-frying or steaming imparts a mellow sweetness to the end result. The alcohol burns off during cooking, much like wine in Western cuisine. You can use Harvey's Bristol Cream sherry as a substitute.

Dried shrimp

Usually found in the chiller or freezer sections of East Asian supermarkets. Like shrimp paste, they will last forever as they have been dehydrated.

Shrimp paste

The *belacan* (shrimp paste) we use at the restaurant is the type that comes in a dense block that's commonly used in Malaysia and Indonesia. I like the brand Jeeny's. It is very strong and flavourful.

I do not pre-toast this block *belacan* for recipes where the shrimp paste is heated during the preparation of a dish (for example in a laksa paste or a cooked sambal like sambal *tumis*).

I generally only use dry-toasted *belacan* for recipes where it goes into a fresh dressing or sambal like the Sambal Belacan (page 108) and the dressing for the Spicy Herbal Salad (page 208). To toast *belacan*, you just need a frying pan or a wok, no oil, and toast, stirring frequently over a low heat until it reaches a dusty, crumbly texture. I highly recommend toasting this in an outdoor space like a garden over a portable gas stove, as the smell is something else and will linger in your home for days, even if all your windows are open! This is the main reason why I decided that the majority of recipes do not require *belacan* to be toasted off. I will usually toast a whole 250g (9oz) block of *belacan* at a time, so that I have a good amount ready to go at a moment's notice.

If you cannot find the block-style paste, jars of Thai Kapi are a good substitute. But note that you will not be able to toast these off in the same way as they contain much more water. If using Thai Kapi for a recipe that requires shrimp paste toasting, add a dash of oil and simply warm it up in a pan to release its fragrance. It will not dry out.

In this book, shrimp paste requirements are given in both teaspoons/tablespoons and in metric/imperial weights because brands and types of shrimp paste vary in consistency. If you are not using the dense block of shrimp paste, you may need to increase the quantity of shrimp paste slightly to match the intensity of the block style.

Soy sauce (dark)

This is used to add a darker, more attractive caramel colour to some dishes, particularly sauces that use cornflour (cornstarch) as a thickening agent.

Soy sauce (light)

Used for its saltiness, my favourite brand is the Japanese Kikkoman. Use any gluten-free light soy sauce if you are gluten intolerant.

Spring onions

The green part of spring onions is more commonly used for finely sliced garnish. I tend to keep the white ends of spring onions to use as a base for simple stir fries.

Tamarind paste

My favourite brand is Namjai as it is the thickest and most concentrated I have found. If using other, more watery brands, you may need to increase how much you use. If you cannot find tamarind paste at all, Lea & Perrins Worcestershire sauce or brown sauce are good substitutes.

Ground white pepper

I often use this in stir fries and in many Chinese dishes.

Yellow bean sauce

My favourite brand is Woh Hup as it doesn't contain artificial MSG. If you cannot find yellow bean sauce, you can substitute it with white miso paste.

MY ESSENTIAL HOME-KITCHEN EQUIPMENT

• Small, medium and large saucepans, a medium wok and a large frying pan. All should be non-stick and have lids. Buy the best quality you can afford – I like Circulon and Le Creuset.

• A good chef's knife or small Chinese cleaver.

• Coloured chopping boards to minimize cross-contamination. At the very least, use two different chopping boards – one for raw meats/seafood, the other for everything else.

• A set of small, medium and large glass mixing bowls.

• Both fine and medium sieves (strainers), and a metal colander.

• A silicon spatula, wooden spoon, slotted spoon, large flat spatula, soup ladle, whisk and metal-ended tongs.

• Chopsticks are a useful makeshift trivet for a wok if you don't own an actual steaming trivet.

• 20cm (8in) square cake tin for steaming rice, taro or radish cakes. Do not use a tin with a loose base for my recipes as the liquids within whatever you're cooking will just leak out!

• A blender or food processor. If you have the room and often cook larger, family-sized portions, an Aimores blender or Magimix XL food processor is great. At home, I use my small Moulinex food processor and a handheld stick blender with stainless steel blades.

• Large melamine plate. In the crockery section at all East Asian supermarkets you will find a plastic melamine selection. I always use a large, oval plate, around 25–30cm (10–12in) in length, to store my *mise en place* from the chopping board. Instead of using several small bowls or plates to hold different ingredients, I just put little piles of chopped garlic, ginger and onions etc. around the melamine plate. This saves a hell of a lot of washing up – a trick I learned from my mother! Melamine is very light so is great for holding just above your pan or wok and using your spatula to push specific ingredients into it. A bonus is that melamine crockery is unbreakable, dishwasher-safe and usually comes in bright, happy colours and patterns to liven up your kitchen.

• Finally, a small noodle basket for quickly and easily blanching ingredients, especially noodles!

SATAY AND MY STREET-FOOD JOURNEY

SATAY AND MY STREET-FOOD JOURNEY

I practised law for several years in London before burning out due to working unsustainably long hours. In the year or two before I burned out, the street-food scene in London was really taking off. I regularly went to Street Feast's night markets in East London and it was here that I first saw Bao. Here were three East Asians, selling beautiful fluffy homemade bao buns, filled with delicious toppings and fried chicken. The queue for their food was always the longest and I think seeing Wai Ting, Erchen and Shing Tat's business sparked a seed of an idea in me. If they could sell food from their heritage and make it a success, why couldn't I?

I realized street food would be a good place, if not the only place, for me to start on my food journey. I had no idea how to open or run a restaurant, and street food resonated with me as it reminded me of the hawker stalls back in Malaysia, each selling just one amazing product, to a happy public. Starting a street-food stall could also be done at a relatively low cost, and so I pounded the streets of London going to as many street-food markets as I could to see what people were selling, how they went about setting up their stalls and which markets had the most footfall. Actual market research!

Malaysian food was the only food that I knew really well and seemed to be massively under-represented in London. At the time, there were only a handful of Malaysian restaurants I knew of in central London. This included the canteen in Malaysia Hall in Bayswater, which is only open to Malaysian passport holders! So, my gut feeling was that there was a gap in the market for good-quality Malaysian food.

At the street-food markets I visited, I noticed that the burger stall would always have the longest queue, which made sense as it was an instantly recognizable product and completely portable, which are important factors for street food. I wanted to sell something that locals would recognize, like a burger, but in a new way with Malaysian flavours. I've never dumbed down the taste of my food, it is always how I would want to eat it, but I generally don't care too much about how things may traditionally be served or made in Malaysia.

The chicken satay burger was born in December 2013. I mixed minced chicken thigh and some egg with a traditional satay marinade and what came out were these awesome juicy burger patties. The first market I sold these at was a Sunday farmer's market in Harringay, north London. It was Wilkes McDermid, a good friend of mine, who argued my case and got me a pitch there. I owe him a lot really, as this market pitch allowed me to really learn the ropes of how to run my fledging business.

This chapter begins with my chicken satay recipe as it was the starting point for everything else that has since followed!

Credit: Giulia Mulè

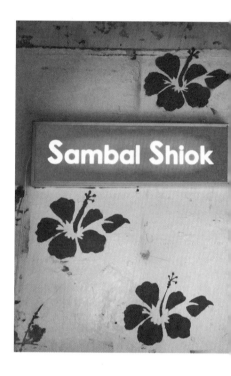

Credit: Wilkes McDermid

Credit: Alexandra Kalinowski

CHICKEN SATAY

SATAY SPICE PASTE
1 lemongrass stalk,
    roughly chopped
600g (1lb 5oz) onion,
    roughly chopped
5 garlic cloves
1 tsp ground coriander
1 tsp chilli powder
1 tsp ground turmeric
½ tsp fennel seeds
½ tsp ground cumin
1 tbsp salt
100g (3½oz) dark
    brown sugar

PEANUT SAUCE
180g (6¼oz) lightly salted
    peanuts, dry-toasted
75g (2½oz) Satay
    Spice Paste
200ml (scant 1 cup)
    coconut milk
60g (2¼oz) dark
    brown sugar
2½ tbsp tamarind paste
¼ tsp chilli powder
150ml (scant ⅔ cup) water
½ tsp salt (or less), to taste

At hawker centres and road-side stalls around Malaysia, you will find people fanning long troughs of smoky charcoal fires, cooking skewers of irresistible slices of meat pre-marinated in lemongrass and spices. The cooks will often use a few stalks of lemongrass tied together as a brush to dab at the meaty skewers to keep the meat moist and crispy. The smell of satay grilled (broiled) over charcoal fire is absolutely irresistible!

In Malaysia, most households have two kitchens – the indoor 'dry' kitchen and the outdoor 'wet' kitchen. Smelly, smoky or oily cooking is sensibly done in the outdoor kitchen. It is usually no more than a lean-to shelter protected from rain and sun by an awning or simple tin roof; one side will be attached to the back or side wall of the main house and the other three sides left open-air. Often the floor will be tiled with a tap and hose conveniently available so that any oil splashes or cooking debris can simply be washed away to leave a sparkling clean floor. I like to think that this outdoor kitchen is referred to as 'wet' because it can easily be hosed down like this! The joy of an outdoor kitchen is that not only is it less of a problem if one makes a bit of a mess while cooking, but also that there aren't lingering food smells because there is plenty of fresh air. Indoor kitchens are only used for cooking non-pungent-smelling foods – definitely no shrimp paste cooking, deep-frying or grilling!

Skewers of chicken satay are a perennial crowd pleaser, and perfect for any summer barbecue. Of course, they can also be grilled indoors, but there is nothing better than satay cooked over smoky flames! Please, please, please use thigh meat for this dish. The slight fattiness adds so much flavour to the end result. Breast meat would simply dry out if cooked this way. This recipe needs to be started at least five hours in advance or the night before to allow for marinating time.

You will end up with roughly double the amount of satay spice paste for the amount of chicken required for this recipe. The satay spice paste keeps very well for up to a month in the fridge and can also be frozen for up to a year. My peanut sauce is runnier than the traditional sauce served with satay because it was originally meant to provide moisture for the chicken satay burger at my street-food stall.

It has been a hit since day one. Both the satay spice paste and peanut sauce are used in every recipe of this chapter.

CHICKEN SKEWERS

1kg (2lb 4oz) skinless and boneless chicken thighs, sliced into 2cm (¾in)-wide strips with those strips then cut into 2.5cm (1in)-long pieces

20 bamboo skewers, soaked in cold water for 10 minutes

3 tbsp oil

1 cucumber and 150g (5½oz) red onion, roughly chopped, to serve

SATAY SPICE PASTE

1. Blend all the ingredients into a fine purée consistency. If using a smaller food processor or handheld stick blender, you will have to work in batches, combining the batches once they're ready. Always mix lemongrass with some onion to provide easier fodder for the blender's blades (blitzing lemongrass by itself can be very hard work and you will be left with undesirable hard, fibrous strands).

PEANUT SAUCE

1. Grind the peanuts using the pulse function of a food processor until you get a rough, sandy texture.
2. Add the ground peanuts, along with the rest of the sauce ingredients, to a medium-sized saucepan. Set over a medium heat and bring to the boil, stirring frequently to prevent the sauce at the bottom of the pan from burning. Reduce the heat to low and simmer for 5 minutes until the sauce thickens.

CHICKEN SKEWERS

1. Marinate the chicken pieces with 150g (5½oz) satay spice paste and refrigerate for at least 4 hours or preferably overnight.
2. Once marinated, skewer on the chicken so that there are five or six pieces per skewer.
3. Drizzle the oil over the chicken skewers.
4. Grill (broil) the chicken on a high heat for 5 minutes, turning frequently to char all sides. You can also use a griddle pan or a barbecue (grill). If cooking indoors, make sure to open all the windows as the charring produces quite a lot of smoke (the smokiness is key to good satay).
5. Serve with peanut sauce, cucumber and red onion.

SATAY BURGERS

CUCUMBER PICKLES
2 cucumbers
400g (14oz) red onions
Pickling liquid:
    350ml (1½ cups) water
    1 star anise
    2.5cm (1in) ginger, sliced
        lengthways into 3 or
        4 pieces
    125g (4½oz) white sugar
    75ml (⅓ cup) white
        rice vinegar
    1½ tsp salt

SIMPLE CHILLI SAUCE
60g (2¼oz) dried chilli
    (red pepper) flakes
2 tbsp dark brown sugar
½ tsp salt
420ml (1¾ cups) water

CHICKEN SATAY PATTIES
500g (1lb 2oz) boneless
    skinless chicken thigh,
    minced in a food
    processor
75g (2½oz) Satay Spice
    Paste (page 32)
1 egg, beaten

LENTIL SATAY PATTIES
250g (9oz) moong dal
    lentils, soaked overnight
    and drained
⅛ tsp salt
⅛ tsp cornflour (cornstarch)
75g (2½oz) Satay Spice
    Paste (page 32)

Oil, for frying
4 good-quality burger buns
    (we used to use brioche
    at the stall), to serve
Peanut Sauce (page 32),
    to serve

Right at the start of my journey, Sambal Shiok was described by the *Independent* as 'a clever, enticing offer … ahead of the curve' and by Street Feast as 'hard-hitting Malaysian-inspired street food'. I have my chicken satay burger to thank for these accolades.

At the stall, customers would have the choice to make their burger a double by ordering an extra patty. Many did, and some even went so far as to order triples or, on the rare occasion, a quadruple burger!

I would recommend starting a day in advance before you want to actually cook the burgers so that you can marinate the chicken or soak the lentils, as well as make the cucumber pickles and the simple chilli sauce. The pickles need to be prepared at least one day ahead for the onions to turn pink and will last for a week in the fridge once drained. These easy cucumber pickles have been on my menu since day one as they remind me of the pickle eaten with *murtabak roti* (flaky flatbread stuffed with curried mutton). Pickling the onions turns them an attractive pink colour.

The simple chilli sauce (sambal *oelek*) is useful to have around to add a clean chilli hit to whatever you are cooking.

You can choose to make either the chicken or lentil satay patties. Finally, this recipe assumes that you have already made the Satay Spice Paste and cooked the Peanut Sauce (both on page 32)!

CUCUMBER PICKLES

1. Bring the pickling liquid ingredients to the boil, then turn off the heat. Remove the ginger and star anise from the liquid.
2. Cut the cucumbers in half straight through the middle, and then halve again lengthways. Use a spoon to deseed them and finely slice so that you end up with crescent moon shapes, ideally no thicker than 5mm (¼in).
3. Cut the red onion into eighths, then slice them so that you also end up with crescent moon shapes, ideally no thicker than 5mm (¼in) in width.
4. Mix the cucumber and red onion thoroughly in a large bowl before decanting into a storage container.
5. Pour pickling liquid over the prepared vegetables and leave at least overnight before draining thoroughly.

SIMPLE CHILLI SAUCE

1. Add all the ingredients to a medium saucepan and bring to the boil. Switch off the heat and leave for 1 hour.

2. Bring to the boil again and simmer over a medium heat for 15 minutes.

Turn off the heat and use a hand blender to blend into a sauce.

CHICKEN SATAY PATTIES

1. Using a gloved hand, mix the chicken mince thoroughly with the satay spice paste and egg in a large container. Leave to marinate in the fridge for at least 4 hours or overnight.

2. Place a large frying pan over a medium–high heat, adding just enough oil to coat the bottom of the pan.

3. Using a large ice-cream scoop, scoop out two balls of the chicken mix into the pan and flatten into patties using a flat spatula.

4. Pan-fry the patties on both sides for around 8 minutes in total, flipping every couple of minutes.

LENTIL SATAY PATTIES

1. These became my vegan version of my chicken satay patties at the stall. They are best eaten within 10 minutes of being cooked as they harden as they cool.

2. Blitz the drained lentils, salt, cornflour and satay spice paste in a food processor until it's a fine paste. (This mixture will store well refrigerated in an airtight container for up to a week.)

3. Place a large frying pan over a medium heat, with enough oil to coat the bottom of the pan.

4. Using a large ice-cream scoop, scoop out two balls of the lentil mix into the pan and flatten into patties using a flat spatula. You may be able to fit more into your pan depending on how large it is.

5. Pan-fry the patties on both sides for around 5 minutes in total, flipping every minute.

ASSEMBLING THE BURGER

1. Cut the buns in half and toast cut-side down.

Then add the toppings to the bun base in this order:
- Peanut sauce (enough to cover the base of the bun)
- Cooked chicken or lentil satay patty
- 2 tablespoons cucumber pickles
- 1 tablespoon simple chilli sauce (or more, to taste)
- Top of bun.

2. Eat!

SERVES 4

MALAYSIAN FRIED CAULIFLOWER

1 cauliflower
75g (2½oz) Satay Spice
    Paste (page 32)
Spiced Flour Mix (page 38)
300ml (10½fl oz) coconut
    milk
Oil, for frying

Peanut Sauce (page 32),
    to serve

The vegan version of our beloved fried chicken (see following page) was born at the restaurant when Tom Kerr replaced the chicken with lightly roasted cauliflower and the egg with coconut milk. Genius!

1. Preheat the oven to 170°C/150°C fan/325°F/gas mark 3. Strip the leaves from the cauliflower and then wrap the whole cauliflower in foil. Par-roast for 45–60 minutes – the cauliflower is ready when you can easily slip a knife into the stalk.
2. Cut the cauliflower into 5cm (2in)-wide pieces, cutting larger florets in half and using more of the stalk to bolster the size of smaller florets.
3. Mix the florets with the satay spice paste, making sure that they are all evenly coated.
4. Heat at least 5cm (2in) of oil in a large pan until it reaches 190°C (375°F).
5. Combine the spiced flour mix in a bowl, mix well, then transfer to a shallow dish. Add the coconut milk to another shallow bowl.
6. Dredge the florets in coconut milk and then in the spiced flour mix, then repeat both. Shake off any excess flour. Do this as close as possible to frying, otherwise the florets will become sticky.
7. Fry the florets in small batches for 3 minutes. Do not overcrowd the pan otherwise the temperature will not be maintained. Turn halfway through to ensure even cooking.
8. Rest the fried cauliflower on a cooling rack as the pieces will crisp up once cooled a little. Allow the oil temperature to increase back to 190°C (375°F) before frying the next batch.
9. Serve with peanut sauce.

MALAYSIAN FRIED CHICKEN

500g (1lb 2oz) boneless, skinless chicken thighs, cut into 2.5cm (1in)-wide strips
75g (2½oz) Satay Spice Paste (page 32)

SPICED FLOUR MIX
250g (9oz) gram flour
1½ tsp salt
1½ tbsp ground coriander
1½ tbsp chilli powder
1½ tbsp ground turmeric
2 tsp fennel seeds
2 tsp ground cumin

3 eggs, beaten
Oil, for frying

Peanut Sauce (page 32), to serve

This is the most popular snack at the restaurant – who can resist fried chicken?!

My starting point is, of course, chicken satay, fresh and dripping with charcoal smoke, dipped into peanut sauce, which is found everywhere in Malaysia. Charcoal grilling (broiling) presents much more of a challenge in the UK's cold, wet climate, so here I use my satay spice paste to marinate strips of chicken thigh (affectionately known as tenders), then dredge them in egg and then a spiced gram flour coating before frying. I use gram flour (a flour made from chickpeas) to make the recipe gluten free, meaning I can serve it to as many people as possible, without needing to adapt the recipe for those avoiding gluten. I'd come across gram flour used in Indian dishes such as *vadai* (savoury doughnuts) so I knew that it was extremely flavourful.

This recipe needs to be started at least five hours in advance or the night before to allow for marinating time. You MUST use chicken thighs for this recipe for maximum juiciness. This yields crunchy, crispy chicken tenders, supremely fragrant and tasty from their satay marinade. Biting into a juicy piece of my fried chicken is heaven in itself, or you can serve them with the Peanut Sauce (page 32) as a bonus!

1. Marinate the chicken in the satay spice paste for at least 4 hours, or preferably overnight.
2. Combine all the ingredients for the spiced flour mix in a bowl, mix well, then transfer to a shallow dish.
3. Add the beaten eggs to another shallow dish.
4. Heat at least 5cm (2in) of oil in a large pan until it reaches 190°C (375°F).
5. When you are ready to fry, prepare the chicken (if you do so too far in advance, the chicken will become sticky). Using gloved hands, first dredge the chicken in the egg and then through the flour mixture. Shake off any excess flour.
6. Fry the chicken pieces in small batches for 90 seconds until golden brown. Do not overcrowd the pan, otherwise the temperature will not be maintained. Turn halfway through to ensure even cooking.
7. Rest the fried chicken on a cooling rack – the pieces will crisp up once cooled a little. Allow the oil temperature to increase back to 190°C (375°F) before frying the next batch.
8. Serve with peanut sauce.

PEANUT GADO GADO SALAD

60ml (¼ cup) white rice
    vinegar
60g (2¼oz) white sugar
200g (7oz) carrot, sliced
    into fine matchsticks
30g (1oz) red onion,
    finely chopped
½ cucumber
100g (3½oz) potato, cut into
    1cm (½in) cubes
3 tbsp oil
Small handful of coriander
    (cilantro) leaves
200g (7oz) Peanut Sauce
    (about half of the recipe
    yield on page 32)
2 eggs, hard-boiled for
    7½ minutes, peeled and
    cut into quarters
    lengthways
Handful of lightly salted
    cassava, or potato
    crisps (chips)

This is the secret sleeper on the restaurant's menu and hasn't
changed since we opened. It is very unassuming and many overlook it
for the sexier Malaysian fried chicken on our snacks section. However,
once you've tried this salad, full of different textures and crunch, you
will be hooked.

At the restaurant we don't serve it with the egg, as is the norm
back in Malaysia, as we don't want it to be too filling. It therefore
becomes a perfect vegan vehicle for our peanut sauce, fresh with lots
of vegetables and zingy from the pickled carrot. When people eat this
salad, the small, crispy squares of potato are often mistaken for the
more traditional fried tofu.

You only need two tablespoons' worth of the pickled carrot for this
recipe, drained from its pickling liquid. It keeps very well for up to a
month in the fridge so you can happily add it to other salads, stir fries
or sandwiches for a kick of flavour.

Before our Covid-19 closure, we never offered takeaway at
the restaurant, as we did not have the space to store disposable
containers and were often too busy during service to handle takeaway
orders. We had a lovely customer, Amanda, come in without fail every
Saturday lunchtime with her own container just for a takeaway of this
salad. This should tell you how good it is!

1. First, make a simple pickle. Warm up the vinegar and sugar in a
small saucepan, warming just enough to melt the sugar. Pour over
the julienned carrot and leave for at least an hour.
2. Next prepare the other vegetables. Soak the chopped red onion in
cold water for at least 15 minutes, then drain. Cut the cucumber in
half lengthways and use a spoon to deseed. Finely slice so that you
end up with crescent moon shapes, ideally no thicker than 5mm (¼in).
3. Parboil the potato cubes for 3 minutes before draining and leaving
to cool. Once cool, pan-fry in 3 tablespoons of oil over a medium–
high heat until crispy.
4. Place 2 tablespoons of the carrot pickle, red onion, cucumber and
fried potatoes, along with the coriander leaves and peanut sauce,
into a mixing bowl. Mix well to combine before transferring to a
serving plate.
5. Place the egg quarters on the plate around the salad. Gently crush
the crisps with your hands and sprinkle over the salad.
6. Eat immediately, as the vegetables will go soggy if left in the sauce
for too long.

HAWKER-CENTRE FAVOURITES

The basic standard of food available throughout Malaysia is astonishingly high. Everything is supremely tasty and deeply satisfying. Malaysians live for food. Class barriers or differences do not exist in the quest for good, satisfying food. And this is really available to everyone, at all budgets. We eat at least five times a day: breakfast, lunch, tea-time, dinner, supper and many snacks in between. Lunch is always a hot meal as it would be sacrilegious to waste a meal with anything cold or nondescript. Every mealtime is an event.

Hawker centres, food courts and coffee shops (affectionately known as *kopi tiams*) are the most common way of eating in Malaysia throughout the day. Most *kopi tiams* usually have a few hawkers selling their specialities. Each hawker (stall-holder) will specialize in just one or two dishes. Occasionally, a hawker may have been selling the same thing over a span of 30, 40 or even 50 years, often passing the business on to their children. A popular hawker may have a long queue of people waiting patiently for their food as soon as the stall opens! Food courts operate in the same vein by collecting many hawkers in one place, which makes it a very convenient way of eating.

An owner of a *kopi tiam* will tend to run the drinks stall and will rent out stalls within their coffee shop to hawkers. It is a happy, mutually beneficial relationship! Most coffee shops will usually have a *char kway teow* purveyor (wok-fried flat rice noodles), a laksa purveyor and possibly a chicken rice/noodle soup purveyor, at the very least.

As a side note, in Malaysia there are, of course, Western-style coffee shops that sell tea, coffee, cakes and other sweet treats.

You cannot miss a hawker centre, food court or *kopi tiam* in Malaysia as there will be one round the corner or in the nearest mall. Walking into one, you will be instantly hit by a cacophony of noise – hawker-stall owners shouting out orders to their helpers, the flash of metal ladles on hot woks, gas burners firing up, customers talking excitedly among themselves anticipating their meals to come, drinks orders being taken, bills being settled with ringgit dollar notes. Then the heat and delicious smells will hit you – spring rolls and noodles frying, fragrant soups simmering away, the smell of sambal chilli sauce and calamansi lime being squeezed into multiple laksas. Last but not least, you will be overwhelmed by everything you see going on around you – crispy roast pork being chopped up, flames from massive charcoal grills licking endless skewers of satay, more flames underneath woks frying noodles and claypots braising fish-head curries.

This section contains my rendition of my favourite hawker-stall meals and, of course, the laksas served at the restaurant.

COCONUT RICE WITH EGG AND SAMBAL

SAMBAL TUMIS
10 dried red chillies or
    2 tbsp chilli (red pepper)
    flakes
200g (7oz) onion, roughly
    chopped
2 garlic cloves
8 red chillies, roughly
    chopped
200ml (scant 1 cup) oil
1 lemongrass stalk, cut
    in half then pounded
    lightly with a pestle
    to bruise
1 tbsp dark brown sugar
1 tbsp tamarind paste
25g (1 tbsp) shrimp paste

FRIED ANCHOVIES
100g (3½oz) dried
    anchovies
Oil, for frying

COCONUT RICE
350g (12oz) long grain or
    jasmine rice
330ml (4fl oz) water
290ml (1¼ cups) coconut
    milk
¾ tsp salt
1 pandan leaf, washed,
    dried and tied into a knot

ASSEMBLING THE PLATES
4 eggs
½ cucumber, finely sliced
200g (7oz) peanuts,
    toasted in a dry pan and
    then lightly salted

Called *nasi lemak* in Malaysia, *nasi* is 'rice' and *lemak* means 'fatty' or 'rich', from being cooked in coconut milk. This is one of our national dishes.

Nasi lemak refers to this entire dish: coconut rice with lots of accompaniments – traditionally, slices of fresh cucumber, salty *ikan bilis* (dried anchovies) fried until crispy, lightly salted toasted or fried peanuts, eggs (hard-boiled, soft-boiled or fried), and last but certainly not least, sambal *tumis* (cooked sambal) to bring it all together.

The magic of *nasi lemak* is that you are able to have a different range of flavours and textures in every single mouthful from taking a little bit of each of the condiments. Malaysians do love variety, even in a single meal.

I would say that you MUST have at least coconut rice, eggs and sambal *tumis* for the dish to be counted as *nasi lemak*!

Sambal *tumis* is very versatile and can be used for many other dishes or just with a fried egg on toast! More traditional recipes will call for all of the ingredients and seasonings to be simmered together. In the restaurant we've found that cooking down the onion mix first really helps to prevent anything sticking to the bottom of the pan, because it is really the sugar that is the sticky culprit. So, I now use this method at home too, as I generally prefer an easier life. To make it vegan, simply replace the shrimp paste with an equal amount of salt.

In Malaysia, anchovies of many different sizes are pulled out of the sea and left to dry in the tropical sun for several days until they are preserved in their natural salt. We know them as *ikan bilis*. At the restaurant we have used frozen Chinese silver fish as a substitute. They are not salty like *ikan bilis* though, and so need a light sprinkle of salt immediately after frying to mimic the traditional taste. To make a vegetarian *nasi lemak* simply use crushed, lightly salted cassava or potato crisps (chips) instead of fried anchovies.

SAMBAL TUMIS

1. Start by cooking the sambal – it can even be cooked the day before and keeps well refrigerated for up to two weeks. Soak the dried red chillies or chilli flakes in more than enough water to cover them, using water that has just boiled. Leave for 15 minutes then drain.

2. Blitz the onion, garlic, chillies and rehydrated dried chillies until the consistency of a smooth paste is achieved.

3. Heat the oil in a wok or large saucepan over a medium heat. Stir-fry the onion mixture and lemongrass for 10 minutes, stirring often. Make sure your windows are open as the chillies will start to smoke!

4. Add the dark brown sugar, tamarind and shrimp paste. Continue stir-frying for another 5 minutes until fragrant and the oil separates. Remove the lemongrass and it is ready for use.

FRIED ANCHOVIES

1. For the crispy condiment, warm up 2.5cm (1in) of oil in a saucepan to 170°C (340°F) or until a steady stream of bubbles rises from a single chopstick when stood in the oil. Fry the dried anchovies for 1–3 minutes until they become a light blonde, gold colour. If you are using smaller *ikan bilis*, they will take around 1 minute but the larger ones will take longer. Drain on a paper towel to get rid of the excess oil.

COCONUT RICE

1. Use the Cooking Rice recipe (page 82) if cooking the coconut rice on a stovetop, adding the ingredients listed in this recipe instead of plain water. It will also need a longer time to cook – simmer for 25 minutes.

ASSEMBLING THE PLATES

1. While the rice is cooking, bring a small pan of water to the boil. Lower in the eggs gently with a spoon and simmer for 7½ minutes. Then take them out of the pan and place in a bowl under cold running water to stop them cooking. Peel and slice in half.

2. Set out four plates for serving.

3. Once the rice is cooked, place a mound of rice on each of the plates. Then arrange the cucumber, eggs and peanuts around the side of the rice. Put a generous dollop of sambal *tumis* on top of each mound of rice. Finally, add the crispy anchovies on top of the sambal. Serve immediately.

Note: If you are making this for guests who are not confident with chilli, you can serve the sambal and anchovies on the side of the rice instead of on top of it so that they can add the sambal in smaller amounts to their taste as they eat.

HAINANESE CHICKEN RICE

1 whole chicken, as good quality as you can afford (it really will make all the difference to this dish – Fosse Meadows in the UK is my chicken of choice), trim off any excess fat and skin near the cavity and also the parson's nose (this will make dealing with the chicken easier during the cooking process)

3 litres (13¼ cups) water, or however much you need to just cover the chicken in the pot (I use a 1.4kg/3lb 2oz chicken and a pot just large enough to hold the chicken, the water and the aromatics)

5cm (2in) ginger, sliced lengthways

3 spring onions (scallions), washed and cut into 10cm (4in) lengths

200g (7oz) onion, chopped into quarters

2 garlic cloves

GINGER CHILLI SAUCE

6 red chillies, roughly chopped

8 garlic cloves

5cm (2in) ginger, roughly chopped

1 tbsp white sugar

1 tbsp white rice vinegar

½ tsp salt

60ml (¼ cup) oil

Splash of chicken stock (bouillon) and soy sauce (optional)

This is a comforting, homely dish very close to my heart as my maternal grandfather is from Hainan in the South China Sea, which has a tropical climate like Malaysia. It is more than the sum of its parts. The buttery, garlicky chicken rice, the ginger chilli sauce and the nourishing chicken soup on the side all make it irresistible to East Asians.

Poaching chicken at a low temperature in this way results in beautifully tender, juicy meat. It is normal to see a red blood line running through the breasts; meat closer to the bone will be a dark pink and if you are deft with a cleaver, the marrow in the centre of the bone will be red. The chicken IS cooked, I promise, and the whole point is that it shouldn't be overcooked for this dish.

The fact that you will find variants of this dish all over Southeast Asia is testament to how good it is!

CHICKEN AND STOCK (BOUILLON)

1. First, bring all the ingredients to the boil in a large stockpot or pan, with the chicken breast-side up.

2. Once the water boils, skim off any residue. Use a ladle to turn the chicken so that the cavity is facing up, and then use a pair of tongs to hold the chicken's back through the cavity. Carefully lift the chicken out of the water to pour out the cooler water that is trapped in the cavity. Carefully lower the chicken back into the pot so that it is breast-side up again. Bring the water back up to the boil and cover with a lid. Turn off the heat, and leave the pot covered on the stove for 45 minutes.

3. To check if the chicken is done, lift it out of the pot taking care to drain the cavity of liquid again and put it on a chopping board. Stick a toothpick or skewer into the thickest part of the drumstick; if the juices run clear, it's cooked through. If not, then put the chicken back into the pot, cover and leave for another 10 minutes.

4. When the 45 minutes are almost up, prepare a large ice bath. As soon as the chicken is fully cooked, lift it out of the pot and carefully drain the water from the cavity before lowering it into the ice bath. Leave the chicken in the ice bath for 15 minutes. The ice bath stops the cooking process, locks in the juices, and gives the chicken skin a beautiful silky texture. Then drain the chicken and leave until you are ready to portion and serve. It is completely acceptable to simply carve off the breasts to be thinly sliced, keeping the drumsticks and thighs as larger separate pieces with the bone in. The traditional method of portioning up the chicken requires a steady hand and a sharp Chinese cleaver to cut through the bones. I would prefer that you keep your fingers rather than risk any mishaps with a cleaver!

GARLIC BUTTER RICE
Leftover chicken skin, excess fat and parson's nose
1 tbsp butter
3 garlic cloves, finely chopped
500g (1lb 2oz) rice, ideally jasmine, unwashed
½ tbsp salt
800ml (3½ cups) chicken stock (bouillon), prepared earlier

SOUP
2.1 litres (9 cups) chicken stock (bouillon), prepared earlier
½ tsp white sugar
¼ tsp ground white pepper
2 tbsp salt
2 spring onions (scallions), finely sliced

DRESSING THE CHICKEN
75ml (⅓ cup) light soy sauce
2 tbsp sesame oil
1 tsp ground white pepper
3 spring onions (scallions), sliced finely on the diagonal
Good handful of freshly picked coriander (cilantro) leaves

GINGER CHILLI SAUCE

1. Make the ginger chilli sauce while the chicken is cooking. Blend all the ingredients except the oil, stock and soy sauce, until a fine paste is achieved.

2. Heat the oil in a pan, add the blended paste and fry over a medium heat for 3 minutes until fragrant.

3. Add a splash each of the chicken stock and soy sauce, if available. Or just use a bit of water to dilute the sauce even further if you want it to last longer. It is really strong so don't worry about diluting it!

GARLIC BUTTER RICE

1. Slowly render the excess chicken skin, fat and parson's nose in a medium-sized saucepan over a low–medium heat (no oil is necessary).

2. Once the fat and skin have rendered, remove any crispy skin and the parson's nose. You can lightly salt these and enjoy as a small snack while you're cooking! Then add the butter to the pan. Add in the garlic and stir-fry once the butter has melted. When the garlic starts to brown, its aroma is released and the butter becomes all frothy, add the rice (don't bother pre-washing as the extra water will mess with the water ratio later) and salt. Stir well so that every grain is coated with garlicky fat.

3. Add 800ml (3½ cups) of the chicken stock. Bring to boil on the highest heat with a lid on, then immediately move to the smallest stovetop and simmer on the lowest heat for 20 minutes.

SOUP

1. While the rice is cooking, turn to finishing the soup. Add the sugar, white pepper and salt to the remaining stock. Just before serving, add the spring onions.

Note: There was just over 2 litres (8¾ cups) of stock used for the soup in this recipe. If you have used more water at the start of this recipe because you've used a larger chicken/pot, add more salt to taste. Alternatively, remove any excess stock to use for another recipe like the Chicken and Garlic Noodle Soup (page 60) or the Charred Rice Noodles in Egg Gravy (page 64).

DRESSING THE CHICKEN

1. To portion out the chicken, separate the breasts from the thighs and drumsticks. Cut the chicken breast into slices 1cm (½in)-wide. For ease, you can just leave the thighs and drumsticks as they are. Place all the chicken portions on a large platter.

2. Mix the soy sauce, sesame oil and white pepper. Pour this over the portioned chicken before garnishing with spring onions and coriander.

ANCHOVY FRIED RICE

3 tbsp oil
50g (1¾oz) onion, finely
    chopped
1 tbsp dried anchovies
1 garlic clove, finely
    chopped
50g (1¾oz) white cabbage,
    finely shredded as if for
    coleslaw
2 eggs
200g (7oz) freshly cooked
    rice, or leftover rice which
    has been warmed up in
    the microwave
1 spring onion (scallion),
    finely sliced

SEASONING
1 tbsp light soy sauce
1 tbsp oyster sauce
¼ tsp ground white pepper
1 tbsp Simple Chilli Sauce
    (page 34)

Finely cut chillies in soy
    sauce or fresh Sambal
    Belacan (page 108), to
    serve (optional)

This is a variation of the perennial favourite, fried rice. It is a take
on *nasi goreng kampung* (village fried rice), a dish I have often had
at Malay hawker stalls where *ikan bilis* (dried anchovies) are a key
component. Eating this always takes me back to the Malay uncle
pumping out *nasi goreng* like there's no tomorrow at the hawker
centre at Batu Ferringhi, Penang. To make the recipe vegetarian,
simply leave out the *ikan bilis* and add salt, to taste, at the end of
the cooking process.

1. It is vitally important that all of your rice and vegetable preparation
is done before you start to cook. Keep the wok on the largest
stovetop over the highest heat for the entire process.
2. Add the oil to the wok and place over the highest heat until it is
smoking. Add the onions and dried anchovies. Fry until the fish are
a light golden colour, then add the garlic and cabbage. Stir-fry for
1 minute.
3. Push the ingredients to the side of the wok, leaving a small corner
empty. Crack your eggs into this empty corner, leave for 5 seconds,
then stir-fry to scramble.
4. Add in the rice and seasonings. Stir to incorporate everything and
stir-fry for 5 minutes. Fry for longer if you prefer your rice to have
crispy bits.
5. Garnish with spring onion and if you like, eat with finely cut chillies
in soy sauce or fresh Sambal Belacan (page 108).

PENANG PRAWN NOODLE SOUP

*LARDONS AND
LARD SAMBAL*
250g (9oz) pork back fat
 (optional)
40g (1½ tbsp) shrimp paste
200g (7oz) Simple Chilli
 Sauce (page 34)

*PREPARING THE
PRAWN STOCK*
1kg (2lb 4oz) raw whole
 shell-on king prawns
 (jumbo shrimp) – try to
 pick ones with a lot of red
 tomalley visible within the
 head
60ml (¼ cup) oil
50g (1¾oz) dried shrimp
2 litres (8¾ cups) chicken
 or pork stock
8cm (3in) ginger, cut into
 long slices
125g (4½oz) pork tenderloin
 (optional)

A must-eat if you are in Penang is the prawn (shrimp) noodle soup from 888 Hokkien Mee on Lebuh Presgrave, a stock deep with prawn and pork goodness, livened up by a lard sambal with shrimp and fried lard! We used to have this dish often in KL which resulted in some confusion the first time I visited Penang. In KL, this dish is called *har mee* (literally translated as prawn noodles, *mee* being egg noodles), and in KL there is also another phenomenal dish called *hokkien mee*, which is a mass of blackened egg noodles wok-fried in dark soy and lard. Completely different!

This is a major project which will require two days, as the sambal and the initial prawn stock should be prepared in advance for the flavours to properly develop overnight. Then the day you'd like to eat it, you can simply cook the noodles and toppings, finish the broth and assemble.

If you cannot get pork fat to render into lard, just use store-bought lard. You can, of course, also substitute oil for the lard in this recipe to greatly simplify it. However, rendered crispy lardons of pork fat are one of the tastiest things on this planet, so I would urge you to seek some out for a special weekend project.

LARDONS AND LARD SAMBAL

1. On the first day of your prep, if using the pork back fat, cut it into 2cm (¾in) square pieces and fry over a low heat for 45 minutes until the fat is rendered and you are left with crispy lardons.
2. Place 100ml (scant ½ cup) of the rendered lard in a pan over a medium heat. Add the shrimp paste and fry for 2 minutes, then add the chilli sauce and fry for another 5 minutes until the lard becomes a deep red. Reserve 150g (5½oz) of this lard sambal to use as a condiment; the rest will be added to the broth.

PREPARING THE PRAWN STOCK (BOUILLON)

1. Peel and separate the heads and shells from all the prawns. Use scissors to cut the head away neatly to avoid losing any precious red-head juice, as this is what makes the broth sing. The heads and shells will be used for the prawn stock.
2. Devein the prawn meat for the topping by running a small paring knife along the top of the body of the prawns and then carefully pulling out the intestinal tract. Refrigerate in a container until the next day's blanching of the toppings.
3. Heat up the oil in a large saucepan over a medium heat and fry the dried shrimp for 10 minutes. Then add the prawn heads and fry until they turn orange and the oil turns a deep orange-red.
4. Add the chicken or pork stock to the saucepan. Use a stick blender

Prawn stock (prepared
  earlier)
2½ tbsp Chinese rock sugar
  or 40g (1½oz) white
  sugar
Lard sambal (prepared
  earlier)
2 tbsp salt
1 litre (4⅓ cups) water
250g (9oz) rice vermicelli
Pork tenderloin (prepared
  earlier, optional)
Prawn halves (prepared
  earlier)
50g (1¾oz) morning glory
  (also known as kangkung
  and water convolvulus),
  cut into 5cm (2in) lengths
200g (7oz) beansprouts
5 eggs
500g (1lb 2oz) fresh yellow
  egg noodles
Fried Shallots (page 23)
Crispy lardons (prepared
  earlier)
150g (5½oz) reserved lard
  sambal (prepared earlier)

to pulverize the contents finely. You should see some red-orange
coloured foam on the surface of the stock.

5. Add the ginger, prawn shells and, if using, the pork tenderloin.
Bring to the boil, then cover and simmer over a low heat for
30 minutes.

6. Remove the pork tenderloin, if you've used it, to cool separately
overnight in the fridge.

7. Strain out and discard the shells and other solids from the prawn
stock using a fine strainer. Be sure to really press out the solids with
a ladle so as to not waste a single drop of stock.

8. Let the stock rest, refrigerated, overnight (or for at least 6 hours)
for the flavours to deepen.

FINISHING THE BROTH AND ASSEMBLING THE BOWLS

1. The next day, add the stock, sugar, lard sambal, salt and 1 litre
(4⅓ cups) of water to a large saucepan. Bring to the boil, stirring
frequently to dissolve the seasonings. Turn off the heat once
boiled. Taste and add more salt and/or sugar if necessary.

2. Soak the rice vermicelli in 2 litres (8¾ cups) of just-boiled water
for 10 minutes.

3. Slice the pork tenderloin, if using, into 5mm (¼in)-thin slices.

4. Bring a medium-sized saucepan of water to the boil. Blanch the
prawns for 60 seconds in the boiling water using a slotted spoon.
Do this in small batches as the prawns need to cook quickly. Remove
from the pan and cool.

5. The prawns should now be cool enough to handle. Carefully cut
them into half lengthways through the body so that you are left with
semi-circles, ready for serving.

6. In a separate small saucepan, soft-boil the eggs for 6½ minutes,
before removing from the pan into a bowl under running cold water
to cool. Peel and cut in half.

7. When it is time to serve, return the prawn broth to the heat while
you bring everything together.

8. Assemble five bowls with portioned-out vermicelli, egg noodles,
morning glory and beansprouts. Blanch the contents of each bowl
in the reserved hot water at a rolling boil for about 15 seconds (a
noodle basket is the best utensil for doing this) – this will make all
the toppings piping hot again and also remove the alkaline smell of
the egg noodles. Lift the noodle basket out from the water and drain
the water thoroughly by jerking the noodle basket sharply downwards
and shaking. Put the hot noodles and vegetables back into the bowl.
Repeat until all the bowls have been reheated.

9. Divide up and arrange slices of prawns and pork (if using) among
each bowl. Top with the hot prawn broth.

10. Garnish with eggs, fried shallots and crispy lardons, and serve
immediately with the reserved lard sambal on the side.

CHICKEN AND GARLIC NOODLE SOUP

Kway teow th'ng is our version of chicken noodle soup. Warming and nutritious, it has lots of different textures to excite your palate. The magic to this dish is the smell of the garlic oil when you first tuck in.

The simple green chilli pickle is found everywhere at Chinese hawker stalls and goes especially well with won ton noodles, Chinese roast meats with rice and Charred Rice Noodles in Egg Gravy (page 64) – basically with any dish which is on the more neutral, non-spicy side of things! You'll need to make this pickle the day before and it will last for weeks in the fridge.

PICKLED GREEN CHILLIES

1. Add the vinegar to the salt and sugar, and stir together to dissolve them. Place the chillies in a glass container or Kilner jar. Cover with the pickling liquid and leave overnight.

CHICKEN STOCK (BOUILLON)

1. Add the chicken wings, water and aromatics to a large stockpot or pan and bring to the boil. Once it comes up to the boil, skim off any impurities and then simmer on the lowest heat, covered, for 90 minutes. Remove the solids, passing the stock through a fine strainer.
2. Remove the meat from the wings and reserve, discarding the chicken skin and bones.
3. Add the sugar, salt and pepper to the soup, stir to dissolve and adjust, to taste.

ASSEMBLING THE BOWLS

1. Cook the dried rice sticks according to the instructions on the packet. If using fresh ho fun, separate out the noodle strands.
2. Bring the soup to the boil and add the fishball halves. Simmer for 2 minutes then turn down the heat to very low, just to keep it hot.
3. To assemble the dish, distribute the cooked noodles and bean-sprouts across four bowls. Add a small handful of shredded chicken.
4. Turn up the heat of the soup to medium–low. Blanch the contents of each bowl in the hot soup for about 15 seconds (a noodle basket is the best utensil for doing this) – this will make all the toppings piping hot again. Lift the noodle basket out from the water and drain the water thoroughly by jerking the noodle basket sharply downwards and shaking. Put the hot noodles and toppings back into the bowl. Repeat until all the bowls of noodles have been reheated.
5. Add 4 fishball halves to each bowl and then distribute the hot soup among them.
6. Finish each bowl with a tablespoon of garlic oil, a teaspoon of fried shallots and a sprinkle of spring onion greens. Serve with the pickled green chillies in some light soy sauce on the side.

PICKLED GREEN CHILLIES
300ml (10½fl oz) white rice vinegar
1½ tsp salt
100g (3½oz) white sugar
300g (10½oz) green chillies, finely sliced

CHICKEN STOCK (BOUILLON)
1kg (2lb 4oz) chicken wings
2 litres (8¾ cups) water
5cm (2in) ginger, sliced lengthways
2 spring onions (scallions), cut into 10cm (4in) lengths
200g (7oz) onion, chopped into quarters
1 whole unpeeled bulb of garlic, stabbed with a fork around the sides
½ tsp white sugar
2 tbsp salt
¼ tsp ground white pepper

ASSEMBLING THE BOWLS
400g (14oz) Thai flat rice sticks or 600g (1lb 5oz) fresh ho fun flat wide rice noodles
8 fishballs, (bought from an East Asian supermarket chiller section), each ball cut in half
200g (7oz) beansprouts
Shredded chicken, picked out from all of the wings used to make the stock
60ml (¼ cup) Garlic Oil (page 21)
4 tsp Fried Shallots (page 23)
Handful of spring onion (scallion) greens, finely sliced
Pickled green chillies, to serve
Light soy sauce, to serve

FRIED RICE VERMICELLI

3 tbsp oil

3 garlic cloves, finely
chopped

150g (5½oz) skinless
chicken thigh or breast,
finely sliced (or you can
use any other meat, small
raw prawns/shrimp, or
to make it vegan, use
fried tofu puffs or robust
vegetables like carrots
or green beans)

200g (7oz) rice vermicelli,
soaked in cold water for
at least 30 minutes, then
drained

Large handful of
beansprouts

2 spring onions (scallions),
finely sliced

SEASONING

3 tbsp light soy sauce

1 tbsp oyster sauce (or
replace with ½ tsp salt
to make it vegan)

1 tsp white sugar

½ tsp ground white pepper

1 tbsp water

Fried egg or omelette with
sambal or fresh chillies
in soy sauce, to serve
(optional)

This fried *mee hoon* rice vermicelli is a popular addition to any meal, and from a busy parent's perspective a godsend as it provides a quick, no-fuss, one-pot meal. My mum used to make this often and you will find this at many hawker stalls, available at all times of the day, in Malaysia.

It is also a perfect dish for any potluck or dinner parties as it can be scaled up and cooked a day or so in advance, and simply warmed up in a microwave before tucking in.

1. Add the oil to a wok and place over a high heat; let it warm up for at least 1 minute before adding the garlic. Stir-fry quickly and then add the chicken, cooking for 1 minute, stirring frequently.

2. Add the rice vermicelli and seasoning. Stir-fry for 3–5 minutes depending on how dry you like your noodles. Finally add the beansprouts and spring onions. Stir-fry for another minute to incorporate everything.

3. This works well served with a fried egg or thinly sliced omelette, as well as any sambal or finely cut chillies in light soy sauce.

CHARRED RICE NOODLES IN EGG GRAVY

160g (5¾oz) Thai dried flat
  rice sticks or 300g
  (10½oz) fresh ho fun flat
  wide rice noodles
3 tbsp oil
1 tbsp dark soy sauce
4 garlic cloves, finely
  chopped
500ml (2 cups) chicken
  stock (bouillon)
1 tbsp cornflour
  (cornstarch), mixed with
  2 tbsp water to form a
  slurry
2 eggs
Pickled Green Chillies
  (page 60) or finely sliced
  fresh chillies in light soy
  sauce and pinch of sugar,
  to serve

SEASONING
1 tbsp oyster sauce
1 tsp light soy sauce
1 tsp ground white pepper
⅛ tsp white sugar

I perfected this recipe during the first Covid-19 lockdown. When
it become glaringly obvious that overseas travel would be out of
bounds for an indeterminable length of time, I found myself craving all
of the hawker-centre dishes. Especially *wat tan hor* which translates
more or less to '*ho fun* noodles in silky-smooth egg' – a very aptly
named dish. I had never cooked this before but was pleased at how
straightforward it was to put together. It really is one of the most
comforting dishes and I hope that this will bring you joy on dark days.

TOPPINGS OF YOUR CHOICE

I would recommend one or two robust components like proteins/
sturdy vegetables, and always some form of leafy green. This recipe
uses fishcakes, prawns (shrimp) and bok choy from the list below.
• 10 slices of fishcakes (or substitute with fishballs), found in the
chiller section of East Asian supermarkets.
• Small handful of cooked shredded chicken (or substitute with
sliced tofu puffs, fried firm tofu or pre-blanched sturdy vegetables
like carrots or green beans).
• 8 raw prawns (or substitute with 3 tbsp rehydrated dried shrimp
and/or a few squid rings patted dry then cut into bite-sized pieces).
• 2 handfuls of bite-sized pieces of leafy greens like bok choy,
cabbage or choi sum.

1. Cook the dried rice sticks according to the instructions on the
packet. Drain and rinse the noodles in cold water to get rid of excess
starch (don't miss out this step, otherwise the noodles will continue
cooking and then clump up in your wok later). If using fresh ho fun,
loosen them so that they are in individual strands rather than a lump.
2. Heat a wok over the largest stovetop and add 1 tablespoon of oil.
When it is smoking, add the dark soy sauce and noodles, and fry for
a minute until nicely charred. Remove from the pan and set aside.
3. Add the remaining 2 tablespoons of oil along with the garlic to the
wok. Fry until the garlic is lightly coloured.
4. Add your preferred robust toppings (in this case fishcakes and
prawns) and stir-fry until cooked through/warmed up. Then add
the stock and all of the seasoning ingredients. Bring to the boil and
reduce to a simmer once boiled.
5. Add the cornflour slurry. Continue to simmer and once the sauce
has thickened slightly, add the greens and cook for another minute.
6. Then turn off the heat and crack in the eggs. Stir to create an egg-
drop effect and thicken the sauce.
7. Ladle the sauce onto the noodles. Serve immediately with pickled
green chillies or finely sliced fresh chillies in a bit of soy sauce and
pinch of sugar. And you're done!

FRIED FLAT RICE NOODLES

80g (2¾oz) dried Thai flat rice sticks or 200g (7oz) fresh ho fun flat wide rice noodles

2 tbsp oil

3 stalks of Chinese chives, sliced into 5cm (2in)-long batons, or substitute with 2 spring onions (scallions)

2 garlic cloves, finely chopped

80g (2¾oz) prawns (shrimp), cut carefully in half lengthways through the body so that you end up with two prawn semi-circles (this will result in springy, tender prawns)

1 egg

Handful of beansprouts

1 tbsp Sambal Tumis (page 46) or Simple Chilli Sauce (page 34)

SEASONING

1 tbsp kicap manis sweet soy sauce (if you don't have this, then double the quantity of light soy sauce and increase the dark brown sugar to ½ tsp)

1 tbsp light soy sauce

¼ tsp salt

⅛ tsp ground white pepper

¼ tsp dark brown sugar

You will find the best *char kway teow* in Penang sold by hawkers behind their woks atop hellishly hot flames, usually made stronger by a large industrial fan and a powerful extractor hood above them. *Char* means 'fried' and fresh ho fun flat wide rice noodles are also known as *kway teow*, hence the traditional name of this dish.

It is quite difficult to replicate the *wok hei*, or the breath of the wok, on domestic stovetops as it is impossible to get the heat intensity required.

I find this method of frying one portion at a time results in a decent version of the dish. When eating this dish at restaurants in London I have often been disappointed. So, I now generally have this at home when I've cooked it myself so that I can adjust the seasonings to my liking and also leave the noodles untouched in the wok for just a tad too long in order to achieve the charred flavour that I crave in this dish.

You can substitute the prawns (shrimp) with slices of fishcakes, squid rings or chicken breast. To make this recipe vegan, use finely sliced fried firm tofu or tofu puffs and simply leave out the egg.

1. Cook the dried rice sticks according to the instructions on the packet. Drain through a fine strainer and run cold water over them to cool thoroughly (don't miss out this step otherwise the noodles will continue cooking and then clump up in your wok later). If using fresh ho fun rice noodles, loosen the noodles so that they are in individual strands rather than one massive lump. Microwaving fresh ho fun, straight after you've taken them out of the packet, for 30–60 seconds (60 seconds if they are fridge-cold), loosens them perfectly.

2. Mix the seasoning in a bowl so it's ready to throw into the wok later in one fell swoop.

3. Place a wok over a high heat until it is smoking. To achieve any sort of *wok hei*, you MUST fry only one portion at a time. As always, frying rice or noodles is much easier in a wok (yes, it is possible to do so in a frying pan but spillage is unavoidable).

4. Add the oil, garlic and half of the Chinese chives. Stir-fry for a few seconds until the chives have charred a bit.

5. Add the noodles and seasoning. Stir-fry for several minutes until the noodles are charred and have picked up some smokiness from the wok.

6. Now add the prawns and stir-fry for 1 minute.

7. Make space towards the side of the wok, crack in an egg, stir to mix and cook for a few seconds.

8. Finally, add the beansprouts along with the remainder of the Chinese chives and the sambal *tumis* or simple chilli sauce. Stir-fry for 30 seconds and serve hot.

THE LAKSA BAR

It is now no surprise to me that I have ended up building my career around my love of hawker-centre laksas. But how did it happen?

Over the years, my street-food customers would often ask me two questions. Firstly, when was I going to open a proper restaurant so that they could come eat my food in comfort, not in the cold and rain? And also, why didn't I sell laksa?!

In winter 2015, I partnered with Zeren Wilson (a wine expert and ex-sommelier) on our Laksa Nights events showcasing my signature laksa for the first time in the upstairs dining room at The Newman Arms in Fitzrovia in London, paired with a choice of ten different Rieslings by the glass, curated by Zeren. There was so much demand after we sold out for all six sessions in the first week that I started to also serve the laksa in the downstairs pub area, in disposable bowls to walk-ins, so that people didn't miss out.

My experience in Fitzrovia told me that there was definitely a gap in the market for someone to offer a good laksa in London.

Straight after this, in January 2016 we served over 1,500 customers at a two-week pop-up at my friend Colin Tu's restaurant, Salvation in Noodles, in Finsbury Park. Here I expanded my menu to what it is now, including several topping combinations and two types of laksa broth – traditional shrimp as well as a vegan version – rice dishes and snacks. Some nights we served 100–150 customers in just four hours with queues waiting to come in!

I then went on to open two longer-term residencies for six months each. The first long-term residency was at The Sun & 13 Cantons pub, right in the middle of London's Soho. After that we went straight into our second

six-month pop-up at Blend Café in Harringay's Green Lanes. 8 November 2016 is etched in my mind as it was the night of the US election when Barack Obama left the stage, but also the night we received our first-ever visit from a national restaurant critic, Jay Rayner from the *Observer*. What a trip that was! It was a powerful stamp of approval for our fledgling laksa bar.

When I first told my parents I was going to drop law and go into the food industry, they asked me where was the progression, what were my aims and goals? I never really did know or have a master plan. My approach has always been to just do it, to grab opportunities as they come along, to listen to customers, to keep improving, adapting, innovating and pushing myself. A rolling stone gathers no moss, etc. After Rayner's review I had no choice, really, but to open a restaurant and Sambal Shiok Laksa Bar opened in June 2018.

Within the first few weeks of opening, we had been described as 'Holloway's hottest ticket' and been visited by two of the UK's most renowned restaurant critics – Grace Dent and Giles Coren. For two months after those reviews, we had queues twenty-deep outside before we opened, and were packed out until closing time. On one Saturday night in this period, we served 180 in our 40-seater restaurant. Air conditioning hadn't even been installed yet due to planning permission being delayed. It was the height of summer,and temperatures in the open kitchen reached 38°C (100°F). I remember apologizing for the heat to all of the customers sitting at the bar. Everyone just brushed me off, 'Oh it's just like dining in Malaysia'. Laksa had taken off in London in style and I owe it all to this recipe!

SIGNATURE CURRY LAKSA

SPICE PASTE
150ml (scant ⅔ cup) oil
300g (10½oz) onion, roughly
 chopped
8cm (3in) ginger, roughly
 chopped
8 garlic cloves
3 red chillies, roughly
 chopped
15 dried chillies, soaked
 in hot water for
 30 minutes before using
 and then drained
1½ tbsp ground cumin
1½ tbsp ground turmeric
3 tbsp ground coriander
3 tbsp chilli powder
25g (1 tbsp) shrimp paste

LAKSA BROTH
1.7 litres (7¾ cups) chicken
 stock (bouillon)
800ml (3½ cups) coconut
 milk
70g (2½oz) good-quality
 caramelized palm sugar
 or dark brown sugar
2 tbsp salt (or less), to taste
3 tbsp tamarind paste
50g (1¾oz) bunch of laksa
 leaves, or mint or
 coriander (cilantro) as
 a substitute
2 lemongrass stalks, cut in
 half then pounded lightly
 with a pestle to bruise

ASSEMBLING THE BOWLS
6 eggs
12 deep-fried tofu puffs,
 cut into half
120g (4¼oz) green beans,
 cut into 5cm (2in) lengths
200g (7oz) beansprouts
24 king prawns (jumbo
 shrimp), deshelled and
 deveined
600g (1lb 5oz) fresh egg
 noodles
Handful of laksa leaves,
 or mint or coriander
 (cilantro) leaves, finely
 sliced, to garnish

Laksa is one of the most popular hawker-stall meals as it is labour-intensive, though completely possible, to make at home.

It is a classic example of Nyonya cooking and comes in two main variants: the sour assam laksa from Penang and the coconut milk-based curry laksa/laksa *lemak*/curry *mee* from Peninsular Malaysia, Sarawak and Singapore. This dish, at its heart, is a spicy noodle soup.

Malaysians tend to save cooking laksa at home for special occasions due to its time-consuming method and lengthy ingredient list, especially if cooking the chicken or prawn stock (shrimp bouillon) from scratch. The flavour of laksa and other Malaysian recipes is determined by the *rempah* which, in Malay, means spice paste. The *rempah* can be as simple as blitzing up onions, ginger and garlic. Or, at the other end of the scale, the number of ingredients for a *rempah* can run to 20 or more!

This is my signature curry laksa, with a strong chilli and shrimp kick, served at the restaurant. It is based on a *campur*- or *kahwin*-style laksa found in Malacca – a cross between Kuala Lumpur's curry laksa and Penang's fiery assam laksa. The soup has a powerful shrimp base.

The vast majority of the preparation can be done a day or two in advance, like cooking the chicken stock, blitzing and cooking the spice paste, prawns (shrimp) and eggs, and blanching the beansprouts and green beans. The noodles are best blanched just before serving. If you can find them, laksa leaves (ask for *rau ram* or hot mint in Vietnamese supermarkets) add a distinctive fragrance to the dish and take me back to my childhood. Like any good curry, the broth develops in flavour if left overnight.

You can use prawns (shrimp) as big or as small as you like. It is also up to you whether to leave the tails on for presentation purposes.

At the restaurant we substitute shrimp paste with a touch of white shiro miso paste and tomato paste to make the broth vegan. If you would like to make the vegan version, replace the shrimp paste with 1 tablespoon of miso paste and 1 tablespoon of tomato purée, and use vegetable instead of chicken stock. Go wild with your imagination in terms of vegan toppings – at the restaurant we char thin slices of aubergine and small florets of broccoli in the oven before lightly salting them.

I recommend starting this recipe a day before you want to eat it to give the fried-off laksa paste a chance to fully mature overnight, and also especially if making your own chicken stock.

Note: It is perfectly acceptable to use good-quality store-bought chicken stock (bouillon) for this. If making your own chicken stock, make it a day or two in advance to save on the amount of work on the same day! Put 2 litres (8¾ cups) of water into a large pot with a chicken carcass or 1kg (2lb 4oz) of chicken wings, along with 1 star anise, 5cm (2in) ginger sliced lengthways, 3 spring onions (scallions), 200g (7oz) onion chopped into quarters and 2 garlic cloves. Bring to the boil, skimming off residue, and then simmer on a low heat for 90 minutes.

SPICE PASTE

1. Blend all of the spice paste ingredients into the consistency of a fine purée. In a large non-stick frying pan over a medium–low heat, cook the spice paste, continuously stirring for 20 minutes, until it is a rich, dark red-brown colour and the oil separates from the paste. Ideally leave for at least 24 hours in the fridge for the fried paste to develop maximum flavour before using it to make the broth.

LAKSA BROTH

1. Add the laksa broth ingredients to a large saucepan along with the fried spice paste. Bring to the boil, then simmer gently on the lowest heat for 20 minutes. Turn off the heat, then remove the laksa leaves/mint/coriander and lemongrass, and adjust the seasoning (the salt and sugar), to taste. Add the tofu puffs to the broth for 10 minutes so that they soak up the flavour.

ASSEMBLING THE BOWLS

1. I have often been asked how to boil a soft-boiled egg like we do at the restaurant as an additional topping for our laksa. We use medium-sized eggs at room temperature. Start by bringing 8cm (3in) of water up to boil in a saucepan. Lower the eggs into the water with a slotted spoon and turn down the heat so it is at a rolling boil. Set a timer for 6½ minutes for soft-boiled or 7½ minutes for hard-boiled. Once the time is up, immediately take the eggs out, put in a deep bowl of cold water and leave them for 2 minutes to stop the cooking. It is easiest to peel the eggs in water as the water helps to get between the egg's membrane and the shell. Slice in half for prettiness.

2. Fill another saucepan with water and bring to the boil.

3. Whilst the laksa broth is simmering, blanch the following in boiling water one after the other: beansprouts for 10 seconds, green beans for 3 minutes and prawns for 90 seconds. Refresh the beansprouts and beans in cold water immediately after taking out of the boiling water (to stop them cooking in the residual heat), then drain. Remember to allow the water to come back up to the boil before starting to blanch a new ingredient.

4. Finally, blanch the egg noodles for 10 seconds and drain well before distributing among the bowls. Portion everything out into the bowls ready for serving – the beansprouts, green beans and prawns. Pour the hot laksa broth into each of the bowls with 4 halved tofu puffs per serving. Place the boiled egg halves on top and finish with sliced laksa leaves, mint or coriander.

Credit: Kar Shing Tong

PENANG ASSAM LAKSA

SOUP
SPICE PASTE
15 red chillies, roughly
 chopped
150g (5½oz) onion,
 roughly chopped
12 garlic cloves
5cm (2in) galangal,
 roughly chopped
1 tbsp ground turmeric
4 lemongrass stalks,
 roughly chopped
50g (2 tbsp) shrimp paste,
 roughly chopped

4 litres (140fl oz) water
3 lemongrass stalks,
 pounded with a pestle
 to bruise
60g (2¼oz) galangal, halved
 lengthways
1kg (2lb 4oz) whole
 mackerel, cleaned and
 gutted
6 stalks of laksa leaf, stems
 and all (there is no
 substitute for the unique
 fragrance from the laksa
 leaf for this recipe)
80g (2¾oz) tamarind paste
7 pieces of tamarind skin
60g (2¼oz) dark brown
 sugar
1½ tbsp salt

ASSEMBLING THE BOWLS
800g (1lb 12oz) dried
 Penang laksa noodles (or
 1.8mm/¹⁄₁₆in thick round
 Vietnamese bun rice
 noodles)

Spicy, sour, fruity and fragrant, Penang assam laksa noodle soup is regularly voted as one of the most delicious dishes in the world.

'Poached, flaked mackerel, tamarind, chilli, mint, lemongrass, onion, pineapple . . . one of Malaysia's most popular dishes is an addictive spicy-sour fish broth with noodles (especially great when fused with galangal), that'll have your nose running before the spoon even hits your lips.' – **CNN**

Assam or asam means sour in Malay, usually as a result of using tamarind paste. This recipe also uses tamarind skin or peel which comes dried, in thin pieces. It is more sour than tamarind paste, which has a tinge of sweetness to it.

If you've never tried it, its flavours will knock your socks off and are pretty much the polar opposite to a curry laksa. It was Jamie Oliver's favourite dish when he came in for dinner in November 2019 and my dad says it is the best assam laksa he's had outside Malaysia. The latter especially is high praise indeed!

My recipe is based on the assam laksa from the SS2 night market on Monday nights in Petaling Jaya. There are sweeter and also more sour versions but this is how I like it.

SOUP
1. Blend the spice paste ingredients into the consistency of a smooth, fine purée.
2. Put the water, lemongrass and galangal in a large stockpot or pan. Bring to the boil and then add the fish. Return to the boil, then simmer over a low heat, covered, for 15 minutes until the fish is cooked. Transfer the cooked fish to a bowl and let it cool. Discard the bones and carefully peel the skin off the fillets. Flake the mackerel flesh and take care to get rid of any pin bones.
3. Remove the lemongrass and galangal from the fish stock. Add the spice paste, laksa leaves, tamarind paste and tamarind skin, sugar and salt and bring to the boil.
4. Then reduce the heat and simmer, covered, for 30 minutes.
5. Turn off the heat. Taste and add more sugar, salt or tamarind paste to balance the spiciness and sweetness to your liking. Remove the laksa leaves and tamarind skin.

GARNISHES

1 cucumber, deseeded
  and thinly sliced into
  matchsticks
200g (7oz) fresh
  pineapple, cut into small
  pieces 1cm (½in)-wide
200g (7oz) red onion, thinly
  sliced
Handful of mint leaves
3 red chillies, thinly sliced
Handful of laksa leaves,
  finely sliced

CONDIMENTS

2 limes, cut into quarters
Sweetened prawn
  molasses (hey kor/
  Indonesian petis udang),
  diluted with a bit of hot
  water to make it thick,
  viscous but runny. You
  can find the brand Jeeny's
  petis udang in New Loon
  Moon supermarket in
  London's Chinatown and
  also online.

ASSEMBLING THE BOWLS

1. Cook the noodles in a large pot of water on a rolling boil for
10 minutes. Drain and rinse them in cold water to get rid of excess
starch. Place one serving of just-cooked noodles into each bowl,
add some flaked fish and then pour the laksa broth over the top.
2. Top with the garnishes and serve with the condiments on the
side. It is customary for guests to add the diluted prawn molasses to
their own bowls to suit their tastes. I generally like my assam laksa
with a dollop of prawn molasses which fills a Chinese soup spoon!
The molasses should be stirred through the soup to dissolve before
starting to eat, with a squeeze of lime if desired.

HOME-STYLE DISHES

Before I left home for university, I had never really cooked because the kitchen was my mum's domain. I merely enjoyed the fruits of her labour. While a lot of my university housemates subsisted on pasta bakes, sandwiches or beans on toast, I began cooking simple things, like chicken curries, vegetable stir fries, omelettes with onions and oyster sauce, fried fish, fried rice and generally became known among my friends as being a dab hand in the kitchen. I guess that, even though I didn't cook with my mother, I had picked up a lot simply by watching her cook. I had learned little things like knowing how to prepare vegetables for stir-frying, knowing what the oil separating from a spice paste looks like, how to toast shrimp paste before using in a fresh chilli sambal and most importantly, knowing that the secret to most cooking is your *mise en place*, i.e. having everything prepared and weighed out before you start.

While working as a lawyer, I didn't really cook much as I simply didn't have the time.

Things changed when I burned out. I spent three months signed off work resting and recovering. It was during this time that I wrote a list of my favourite dishes from my mum's repertoire and made her teach me, step by step, how to cook them. Dishes like prawn sambal, *bak kut teh* (herbal pork soup), Hainanese pork chop with onion sauce, fried wonton prawn dumplings, fried *meehoon* rice

vermicelli, sweet sticky spare ribs, *yong tau fu* (vegetables stuffed with pork) and *bubur cha cha* (sweet potato and taro sweet soup). I would stand by her side with a notebook, meticulously writing every step down. She would know all the measurements for seasonings by heart, after years of cooking these dishes intuitively. I would physically stop her hand from adding any salt, sugar or other seasoning which she usually did straight from the jar or a glug from a bottle, and make her use a tablespoon or teaspoon as appropriate so that I could accurately record how much of anything was used. Cooking these dishes,

which meant so much to my soul, helped me
to put myself back together and gave me the
strength to start a street-food business.

A typical home-cooked Malaysian meal
involves lots of dishes for sharing, to be eaten
with wonderful plain steamed white rice.
It might include simple braises like Peranakan
pongteh (chicken and potatoes simmered
down with bean paste, soy and shiitake
mushrooms), Peranakan chicken curry *kapitan*,
Indian mutton curry or Malay beef rendang
– slow-cooked curries and stews strong
with spices and deep in flavour. It could be a
comforting soup made with pork ribs and lotus
roots or dried anchovies, or simple stir fries
of *kangkung* (morning glory) with garlic or
shrimp paste. The nation's most beloved
sambal is served on the side, for those who
like their chilli, to pump the heat up a notch.
The rice acts like a flavour sponge, making
sure every single last drop of valuable sauce
is enjoyed.

Hopefully this section will give you
boundless ideas for simple yet satisfying
home-cooked family meals that lend
themselves to batch cooking and freezing, as
well as special feasts or dinner parties. The
beauty of Malaysian food is that you can really
mix and match a wide variety of dishes, such
as pairing spicy with more neutral flavours or
deep-fried ingredients with a braise or a soup.
They will all come together harmoniously, much
like the many races of the country's people.

COOKING RICE (IN A PAN)

I wrote much of this book during the Covid-19 lockdown of spring 2020, in which I spent a lot of time on social media sharing useful tips for cooking at home. The recipe that really engaged people was how to cook rice in a saucepan, what to me seemed to be the simplest, most basic but most important skill.

Unlike many Asians, I do not actually own a rice cooker because I rarely cook for more than two people at home. So, I have perfected cooking rice in a saucepan, and I am pleased to share with you this recipe handed down by Asian mothers to their children. Once you have mastered cooking rice, it is the plain canvas around which you can build a multitude of meals.

People in the West can, it seems, worry about eating leftover rice. However, so long as leftover rice is cooled quickly before being refrigerated overnight and then warmed up until properly steaming when reheating, it is absolutely fine to be eaten within a week (Asians have been doing this forever). Immediately after I finish eating a meal, I decant the rice from the pan straight into a container so that it cools quickly. A good way of ensuring this is to simply rest it on a cooling rack for maximum air circulation. I usually cook more rice than I need so that it is ready to heat up to eat with leftovers the next day or to fry. In fact, I find it key to use pre-cooked and cooled rice to cook fried rice successfully.

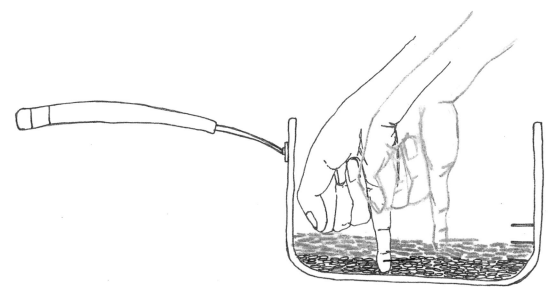

Credit: Marie-Henriette Desmoures

1. You will need a small (15–16cm/6in-diameter) saucepan with a lid. Put 1cm (½in) of uncooked rice into the pan (this is enough for a meal for two people). You can use whatever rice you have: long grain, basmati, jasmine or short grain (just not glutinous, as that requires a different method). This recipe works with white rice, my favourite as it is the best at soaking up tasty sauces.

2. Wash the rice under cold running water – just swivel the pan around then simply pour the water out of the pan. Repeat a maximum of three times as this will be plenty.

3. Here comes the tricky science bit – how to know how much water to add to the pan. Stick your pinky finger into the drained rice. If the rice comes up to the first joint of your finger, then fill the pan with just enough water so that it comes to the first joint of your finger when the tip of your pinky is resting on top of the rice. It is essentially a 1:1 ratio of rice to water using your little finger as a measure.

4. You will need to start the pan off over a high heat on the largest stovetop. Remember to put the lid on as you turn the heat on. Do not walk away yet. Bring the rice to the boil (this is one of the few times I would recommend that you watch a pan come to the boil).

5. As soon as the pan comes to the boil, move it to the smallest stovetop available on the LOWEST heat and leave to simmer, covered, for 15 minutes. Do not take the lid off or stir. Leave it alone to cook!

6. Turn off the heat and leave for another minute or two. Then fluff the rice with a fork, a pair of chopsticks or ideally a rice paddle. If you don't fluff your rice once it's finished cooking, the bottom will crisp up and the rice ends up rather solid without the desired fluffiness.

Note: You mustn't cook more than a third of a small saucepan's worth of raw rice as it will not cook properly. Use the sophisticated finger measurement in a 1:1 rice-to-water ratio. If you want to cook a larger volume of rice, you MUST use a medium-sized saucepan. If you are not adopting the finger method, the proportion of rice to water is 1 cup of rice to 1½ cups of water, with wild or brown rice requiring a bit more water and cooking time.

SOUPS

PORK HERBAL SOUP WITH PRAWN AND MUSHROOM RICE

8 dried shiitake mushrooms, soaked in 400ml (1¾ cups) hot water for at least 30 minutes

500g (1lb 2oz) pork cheek oysters cut into 5cm (2in) chunks

800g (1lb 12oz) pork ribs (those from the chiller cabinets at East Asian supermarkets are best as they tend to be meatier), sliced into individual ribs

2 whole garlic bulbs, pricked with a fork all around the sides

2 sachets herbal soup herbs (I use the brands Teans Gourmet or A1 – some will also come with loose dehydrated herbal strips in which case just add to the soup to infuse with the sachets and remove with a slotted spoon before serving)

1.6 litres (56fl oz) water

14 pieces fried tofu puffs, cut in half

SOUP SEASONINGS

1½–2 tsp salt (depending on your taste – I prefer things very well-seasoned!)

1 tsp ground white pepper

1 tsp ground black pepper

1 tsp white sugar

3 tbsp light soy sauce

1 tbsp dark soy sauce

When I was a child, we used to go to a great *bak kut teh* (pork herbal soup) restaurant in a shop-lot on one of the outer rings of the square main roads in SS2 town centre, a district in Petaling Jaya. I remember it as having an open-air front, with rickety stools and tables made out of metal, set on the pedestrian walkway and the car parking lot right outside the shop. For presentation purposes, the herbal soup would always be served in claypots with lots of accompaniments like sliced fried *you tiao/yau char kwai* (Chinese dough sticks) and fresh-cut chillies. It is one of the great nourishing Malaysian dishes.

This is my mum's recipe for *bak kut teh*. It goes really well with her dried prawn (shrimp) and Chinese shiitake mushroom rice which is her version of the yam rice traditionally served with *bak kut teh*.

This recipe makes a large family-sized amount and I love my mum's addition of pork cheeks as they have a fantastic buttery texture. If you have a smaller household, simply leave out the pork cheeks and halve the other ingredients aside from the ribs – you'll still need at least 800g (1lb 12oz) pork ribs if halving the recipe, as it is the ribs that give the resulting stock (bouillon) its depth of flavour. If you'd like to make a halal version of this dish, feel free to use six to eight skinless, bone-in chicken thighs instead.

This soup is ideal eaten with the prawn and mushroom rice, though plain rice is of course fine, and the Greens with Garlic and Oyster Sauce (page 150).

The prawn and mushroom rice is similar in taste to the Chinese *lor mai gai* (glutinous rice and chicken steamed in bamboo leaves) that you find at dim sum parlours. You could very happily eat leftovers of this with a fried egg, fresh-cut chillies and soy sauce for a quick lunch.

PORK HERBAL SOUP

1. Drain the mushrooms, squeezing well and reserving the water (but not the dirt in the dregs) in a measuring jug. Discard the stalks and then cut each mushroom in half.

2. Add the meat, garlic, mushrooms along with their reserved water, herb sachets, water and soup seasonings to a large stockpot or saucepan. Bring to the boil, then simmer on a low heat, covered, for 2 hours. Alternatively, this recipe really benefits from pressure-cooking (which makes it much, much quicker!) on the highest pressure for 15 minutes.

3. After the 2 hours or 15 minutes (depending on your cooking method), remove the sachets, draining well and squeezing dry like a tea bag so that all the flavourful liquid ends up back in the pot. Remove the garlic bulbs and squeeze out the creamy garlic from their

PRAWN AND MUSHROOM RICE

30g (4 tbsp) dried shrimp, rehydrated in 200ml (scant 1 cup) hot water
4 dried shiitake mushrooms, rehydrated in 400ml (1¾ cups) hot water for at least 30 minutes
2 tbsp oil
150g (5½oz) onion, finely chopped
5 garlic cloves, finely chopped
400g (14oz) rice, unwashed

RICE SEASONINGS

1 tbsp oyster sauce
¼ tsp ground white pepper
¼ tsp white sugar
1 tsp light soy sauce
1 tsp sesame oil
1 tsp salt

Finely cut fresh red chillies in light soy sauce, to serve

skins. Add the fried tofu puffs, leaving them to soak for at least 10 minutes before serving.

PRAWN AND MUSHROOM RICE

1. While the soup is cooking, start to prepare the rice.

2. Soak the shrimp and mushrooms in separate containers for at least 30 minutes. Place a measuring jug on scales and tare the weight to zero. Retaining the soaking liquid and combining in the measuring jug, drain the shrimp and mushrooms well, squeezing every last bit of liquid from them. Check to see how much combined soaking water you have in the measuring jug and add more water so that the total amount of liquid is 840ml (28½fl oz).

3. Discard the stalks of the mushrooms. Finely chop the mushrooms and rehydrated shrimp separately in a food processor. Once chopped, keep in separate containers or in separate piles on a large plate.

4. Warm up the oil in a large saucepan over a medium heat. Stir-fry the onion for 3 minutes until translucent, then add the garlic and fry for a further minute.

5. Add the shrimp and stir-fry for 2 minutes until fragrant.

6. Add the mushrooms and stir-fry for another minute.

7. Add the rice seasonings and reserved soaking liquid, being careful not to pour in the dregs of mushroom dirt in the soaking water. Add the rice (no need to wash as the extra water would mess with the liquid ratio) and stir well to thoroughly combine before putting the lid on and cooking using my method for Cooking Rice (page 82).

8. Once the rice and the soup are both cooked, serve with the fresh red chillies in light soy sauce. The best way to eat this meal is to remove the meat, mushrooms and tofu from your soup bowl onto your plate and drizzle some soy sauce and chillies on top before tucking in with mouthfuls of rice and greens. Drink the comforting soup after every mouthful or two of rice. I often bloat myself by polishing off a dollop of rice added into a final bowl of soup after everyone else has finished eating!

BLACK PEPPER LAMB SOUP

5 tbsp oil
100g (3½oz) onion, halved
    then cut into thick semi-
    circle slices
500g (1lb 2oz) lamb chops
    or ribs

SPICE PASTE
1 tbsp ground coriander
1½ tsp finely ground black
    pepper (or grind up
    1 tbsp black peppercorns
    in a pestle and mortar
    until fine)
1 tbsp salt
1½ tsp fennel seeds
½ tsp ground cumin
1 tsp ground turmeric
60g (2¼oz) ginger, roughly
    chopped
3 garlic cloves

SOUP
1½ litres (6½ cups) water
3 cardamom pods, gently
    bashed with a pestle to
    crack the skin
1 star anise
1 cinnamon stick

GARNISH
Handful of freshly picked
    coriander (cilantro) leaves
Fried Shallots (page 23)

Plain rice or baguette,
    to serve

This is my take on *sup kambing*, literally translated as 'goat soup'. I use lamb for this recipe as it is more commonly available in the UK (lamb is rare in Malaysia, with mutton or goat meat used more often). This soup is perfect for tougher cuts of meat as the cooking time makes it very tender.

This is very warming and perfect for rainy days or cooler evenings. A popular Mamak Indian Muslim dish, my father used to buy it for supper from a push-cart hawker vendor in SEA Park, Petaling Jaya on our night-time or weekend jaunts. You will often find it served with thick chunks of white bread or baguette, lavished with hefty slabs of butter, or margarine as is more common in Malaysia.

You will need to start this recipe several hours in advance or the night before to allow for marinating time. Whatever you do, do not remove any of the fat released from the mutton during the cooking process as that is where all the flavour of this dish lives. This fat is tasty, flavourful and good for you!

1. Blitz all the ingredients for the spice paste into a fine purée.
2. Heat up a medium-sized pan over a medium heat, before adding the oil and onions. Fry for around 5 minutes, until the onions start to turn translucent. Turn the heat down to low and add in the spice paste, stir-frying for no more than 5 minutes, until the fragrance is released. Be careful not to burn the paste otherwise it will have a charred, bitter taste – if necessary, add a splash or two of water to prevent the paste from burning. Pour the mixture into a bowl and leave it to cool for 10 minutes.
3. Rub the cooled spice mixture thoroughly onto the lamb. Cover and marinate in the fridge for at least 4 hours or ideally overnight.
4. Transfer all of the marinated meat into a large stockpot or saucepan, making sure to scrape out every drop of the spice mixture. Add in all the soup ingredients and bring to the boil.
5. Leave the soup to simmer on a low heat, uncovered, for 2 hours. You could also use a pressure cooker, cooking for 15 minutes on high pressure. You'll know it's ready when the meat is so soft that it easily slides off the bone. Taste the soup and add more salt if you think it needs it.
6. Remove the lamb from the soup and strip the meat from the bones for easier eating. Using a slotted spoon, remove the cardamom pods, star anise and cinnamon so that you are left with a clear soup without any bits in it. Add the meat back into the soup before serving.
7. Garnish with coriander leaves and fried shallots. Eat with plain rice or even better, buttered pieces of toasted baguette!

EIGHT TREASURES SOUP

15g (½oz) Korean sweet
  potato glass noodles
1½ tbsp wood ear
  mushrooms or
  dehydrated black fungus
200g (7oz) chicken wings
4 dried scallops (this is
  one of the rare
  ingredients that has to be
  brought back from East
  Asia. You can substitute
  with 3 tbsp dried shrimp,
  which are more readily
  available)
1 litre (4 cups) water
3 dried shiitake mushrooms,
  soaked in 100ml (scant
  ½ cup) hot water to
  rehydrate for at least
  30 minutes
80g (2¾oz) white crab meat
1 egg, beaten
1 tbsp sesame oil
2 spring onions (scallions),
  finely sliced

SEASONING
(mixed together in this
  order)
2 tbsp cornflour
  (cornstarch), mixed with
  2 tbsp water to form
  a slurry
2 tsp dark soy sauce
1 tbsp Shaoxing rice wine
  (optional)
½ tsp ground white pepper
2 tbsp Chinkiang black
  vinegar
Salt, to taste

Additional Chinkiang black
  vinegar, to serve

The 'eight treasures' in this recipe refer to the many ingredients and stock (bouillon) used to make it, and eight is a lucky number for the Chinese, signifying bountiful fortune and prosperity. I served this at my eight-course Lunar New Year feast at Asma Khan's Darjeeling Express in 2018. Every Chinese banquet will always feature a soup. I have fond memories of lavish celebrations with hundreds of guests held at massive Chinese restaurants in Malaysia.

My favourite soup at these banquets used to be shark fin. Of course, I would never eat shark fin now, but my version is so tasty that I don't even miss the original. Shark fin soup was always about the different flavours and textures, in particular the addition of a small final splash of black vinegar before tucking in. It was essentially luxury hot and sour soup!

To shorten the cooking process, you can simply substitute the chicken wings and water in this recipe with a handful of shredded leftover chicken meat and 2 litres (8¾ cups) of chicken stock (bouillon).

If you don't have one or two of the main ingredients below, please do not worry. The important part of this soup is the seasoning so you can really make it with whatever, using as many or as few textural ingredients as you like, or even make it vegan!

1. Soak the glass noodles and wood ear mushrooms or black fungus in the same large container in hot water for at least 30 minutes to rehydrate. The shiitake mushrooms must be rehydrated separately as you will use its soaking liquid later.
2. Put the chicken wings, dried scallops or shrimp and the water in a large saucepan, bring to the boil and then simmer, covered, for an hour.
3. While the stock is cooking, squeeze out the shiitake mushrooms and keep the soaking liquid. Discard the stalks of the shiitake mushrooms and finely slice the mushroom tops.
4. Drain the glass noodles and wood ear mushrooms or black fungus. Finely slice the wood ear mushrooms (the rehydrated black fungus can be left as is). Cut the noodles into roughly 5cm (2in) lengths.
5. After an hour simmering the stock, turn off the heat. If using dried shrimp, you can just leave them in the stock, but remove the wings and scallops. Shred the scallops and the chicken meat, discarding the chicken skin and bones. Return the shredded scallops and chicken meat into the stock.

RECIPE CONTINUES PAGE 94

6. Pour the mushroom soaking liquid slowly into the saucepan of stock, being careful not to pour in any bits of dirt left at the bottom of the container. Add the crab meat, wood ear mushrooms, shiitake mushrooms, glass noodles and seasonings into the stock. Bring to the boil over a medium heat and simmer for 5 minutes to allow the soup to thicken.

7. Turn off the heat and pour in the egg. Stir to create an egg-drop effect.

8. Add salt to taste.

9. Add the sesame oil and garnish with spring onions just before serving.

10. Serve a small bowl of Chinkiang black vinegar for guests to add, according to their taste, to their individual bowls.

SERVES 4–8

SALTED MUSTARD GREENS DUCK SOUP

350g (12oz) salted chilli mustard greens (usually found in vacuum-packed bags in East Asian supermarkets. Drain, discarding the brine and chillies)

3 litres (13¼ cups) water

4 duck legs, skin removed

1kg (12lb 4oz) tomatoes, quartered

SEASONINGS

3 tbsp tamarind paste

6 lemongrass stalks, bruised by pounding lightly with a pestle

120g (4¼oz) ginger, sliced lengthways into long, thick slices

8 Chinese salted plums (from a jar), drained

2 tsp ground white pepper

1 tsp salt

2½ tbsp dark brown sugar

This is a brilliant, comforting soup usually served at Nyonya Lunar New Year family feasts. The preserved mustard greens and tamarind provide the perfect foil to the duck's rich fattiness. It also works very well with chicken if you wish.

This recipe serves 4–8 depending on portion size! How many this will feed depends on whether you're having it as part of a larger meal with a variety of other dishes or whether you're serving the soup just by itself.

1. Cut the mustard greens into thin strips.

2. Add the water, duck legs, sliced mustard greens and all of the seasonings into a large pot. Bring to the boil, then lower the heat, cover and simmer for 1 hour.

3. Add the tomatoes into the pot for the last 10 minutes of cooking.

4. Try the soup and adjust the salt and pepper to taste if necessary.

5. Remove the duck legs from the soup and allow to cool slightly. Shred the meat and add it back into the soup before serving.

MEAT

BEEF RENDANG

SPICE PASTE
2.5cm (1in) piece of
    galangal or ginger,
    roughly chopped
1 tbsp salt
2 tsp chilli powder
600g (1lb 5oz) onion,
    roughly chopped
3 garlic cloves
2 lemongrass stalks,
    roughly chopped
20 dried chillies, soaked
    in hot water for at least
    30 minutes
10 makrut lime leaves,
    stalks removed

3 tbsp oil
1 cinnamon stick
2 star anise
3 cardamom pods, lightly
    bashed with a pestle to
    crack the skin
5 cloves
60g (2¼oz) palm sugar or
    dark brown sugar
3 tbsp tamarind paste
400ml (1¾ cups) coconut
    milk
1kg (2lb 4oz) beef chuck,
    shin or cheek (trim off all
    excess tough sinew and
    cut into 5cm/2in-square
    cubes)
200g (7oz) coconut cream
50g (1¾oz) desiccated
    coconut

Coconut, lemongrass, makrut lime leaves – the smell and taste of rendang is unmistakable for all Malaysians. It is one of our national dishes. Rendang is often served at ceremonial occasions and festivals such as Eid or to important guests – a special occasion warrants the laborious and time-consuming cooking process. It can be eaten simply with steamed rice and sliced cucumbers.

I watched my mother cook rendang often when I was growing up. There are many different recipes for it – most, like my mother's, use *kerisik* (toasted desiccated coconut) but my recipe uses coconut cream instead to achieve a thicker velvety sauce, just adding the desiccated coconut as a garnish instead.

At the street-food stall, I used to serve this beef rendang, sweet pickles and sambal in a brioche bun. My customers told me this was one of the best hangover cures they had ever had! I specifically wanted my beef rendang to have more sauce as I knew that it would go phenomenally well with the bread bun.

This recipe is pretty much unchanged since I first started serving rendang in 2014 at my stalls, and then at the restaurant. Ideally, make it a day before you actually want to eat it, because the flavours really need to cool down in order to come to life. I recommend making more rendang than you need as it only gets better and better with time. Having a portion or two in the freezer is always a winner!

1. When cooking quite a large amount of meat like this, I like to take it out of the fridge for at least an hour before I want to start cooking it, while I'm doing other ingredient preparation, to give it time to reach room temperature. It means that your cooking time will be reduced later.
2. Blitz all the ingredients for the spice paste into a fine purée.
3. In a large pan over a medium heat, add the oil, spice paste, cinnamon, star anise, cardamom and cloves. Fry for a few minutes to release the aromatics.

4. Add the sugar, tamarind paste and coconut milk. Stir to combine and heat for a few minutes.

5. Add the beef cubes. Stir to combine and increase the heat to medium–high to bring to the boil. Then lower the heat to low and cook with the lid on for 2 hours, stirring every few minutes to prevent it sticking to the pan.

6. While the beef is cooking, put the coconut cream in a glass Pyrex jug (or a bowl if you don't have one). Microwave for 2 minutes, stir, microwave for another 1 minute, stir, then microwave for a final minute and stir again. It will end up an aromatic, caramel golden-brown colour. You must stir promptly after every microwaving session as if you leave it for too long without stirring, you will risk the centre of the coconut cream burning which will be disastrous as you will have to start again! Alternatively, you could use a small saucepan (ideally non-stick) to caramelize the coconut cream. Heat it up over a medium–low heat, stirring constantly, until it is golden brown.

7. Use a non-stick frying pan to dry-toast the desiccated coconut for a few minutes until it is light brown, which you will use for garnish.

8. After the beef has been cooking for 2 hours, add the caramelized coconut cream to the pan and then cook with the lid on for 30 minutes, stirring every few minutes. Then take the lid off and simmer on a low heat for a final 30 minutes, stirring frequently to prevent the sauce sticking to the bottom of the pan.

9. Garnish with toasted desiccated coconut sprinkled on top.

Note: Instead of the total 3 hours slow-cooking method given above, you can really speed up this recipe by pressure-cooking on high for 22 minutes, then adding the caramelized coconut cream before simmering on a low heat for 30 minutes to reduce the sauce. You'll still need to stir the sauce frequently towards the end to prevent it sticking to the bottom of the pan.

MALAYSIAN CHICKEN CURRY

75ml (⅓ cup) oil

200g (7oz) onion, roughly chopped

3 tbsp meat curry powder (if you don't have this, combine 1½ tsp chilli powder, 1½ tsp ground coriander, ¾ tbsp finely ground black pepper, 1 tbsp ground turmeric and 1 tsp ground cumin)

6 skinless, bone-in chicken thighs (cooking chicken on the bone enriches your final curry. Please never use breast!)

200ml (scant 1 cup) water

200g (7oz) canned chopped tomatoes or fresh tomatoes, roughly chopped

300g (10½oz) potatoes, cut into chunks approximately 4cm (1½in) wide

1 tbsp salt

1 tbsp white sugar

100ml (scant ½ cup) coconut milk

This is a dish that every Malaysian household will make in its own way, and this one is based on my mum's recipe. Malaysian chicken curry is mild–medium in terms of chilli heat, creamy from coconut milk, tangy from tomatoes, and best of all are the potatoes which have been cooked in the curry sauce. Any leftover sauce will go very well with leftover rice and a fried egg or two.

We often use ready-made curry powders, and my favourite brand is Adabi from Malaysia. I have included a DIY version.

1. Pour the oil into a large saucepan over a medium heat and fry the onions for 5 minutes.

2. Add the curry powder, stir and carry on cooking for 3 minutes, reducing the heat a little to medium–low.

3. Add the chicken thighs and stir until all the chicken is coated.

4. Pour in the water and tomatoes. Increase the heat and bring to the boil, then add the potatoes.

5. Add the salt, sugar and coconut milk. Return to the boil, then reduce to a simmer for 30 minutes, turning over the chicken pieces every now and then. And it's as simple as that!

SERVES 4

MALAY RED CHICKEN

6 skinless, bone-in chicken
    thighs
1 tsp ground turmeric
1½ tsp salt
3 tbsp oil
1 star anise
3 cloves
1 stick cinnamon
2 cardamom pods, lightly
    bashed with a pestle to
    crack the skin slightly
100g (3½oz) canned
    chopped tomatoes or
    fresh tomatoes, roughly
    chopped
100g (3½oz) tomato
    ketchup
100ml (scant ½ cup) water
80g (2¾oz) frozen peas
Handful of picked mint
    leaves and juice from
    ½ lime, to garnish

SPICE PASTE
200g (7oz) onion, roughly
    chopped
4 garlic cloves
2 lemongrass stalks,
    roughly chopped
5cm (2in) ginger, roughly
    chopped
2 red chillies, roughly
    chopped

Ayam masak merah (red cooked chicken) is a beautiful Malay
dish usually reserved for celebrations like weddings and Eid. This
comforting dish doesn't have too much chilli so is popular with
everyone, young and old. It uses the traditional Malay *empat sekawan*
(four friends) of cinnamon sticks, cardamom, star anise and cloves.
Browning the chicken thighs seals in flavour before it is added to the
rich gravy to cook it through. It goes very well with the Spicy Herbal
Salad (page 208), as the salad will add a welcome fresh tartness to
your meal.

1. Marinate the chicken with the ground turmeric and salt. You can
do this the night before and leave the meat in the fridge overnight
to marinate. However, I usually just do it on the day of cooking and
simply leave the marinating chicken for an hour in its bowl on the
kitchen counter to give it time to reach room temperature. It means
that your cooking time will be reduced later.
2. Blitz the spice paste into a fine purée.
3. Heat up the oil in a large pan over a medium–high heat. Brown the
chicken for a minute or so on each side. Remove the chicken from the
pan onto a plate.
4. Turn the heat down to medium and fry off the spice paste along
with the star anise, cloves, cinnamon and cardamom, stirring often,
until the oil separates and the onion has turned a luscious caramel
colour (this will take a maximum of 10 minutes).
5. Add the chicken pieces, any excess oil left on the plate, tomatoes,
ketchup and water. Bring to the boil, then reduce the heat, cover,
and simmer for 25 minutes. Add the peas for the last 10 minutes of
cooking. Turn off the heat, taste and add more salt if desired.
6. Garnish with mint leaves and a squeeze of lime.

NYONYA CHICKEN CURRY KAPITAN

6 skinless, bone-in chicken
    thighs
70ml (2¼fl oz) oil
300ml (10½fl oz) water

MARINADE
1½ tsp ground turmeric
1½ tsp salt
2 tbsp oil

SPICE PASTE
200g (7oz) onion, roughly
    chopped
2 garlic cloves
5cm (2in) ginger, roughly
    chopped
1½ tsp ground turmeric
2 lemongrass stalks,
    roughly chopped
120g (4¼oz) red chillies,
    roughly chopped
10g (1 tsp) shrimp paste

SEASONINGS
200ml (scant 1 cup) coconut
    milk
100g (3½oz) canned
    chopped tomatoes or
    fresh tomatoes, roughly
    chopped
1 tbsp tamarind paste
2 tbsp dark brown sugar
4 makrut lime leaves
1 cinnamon stick

This is probably the king of the chicken curries you will find in Malaysia. It is a step up from the much-loved chicken curry with potatoes made by all households up and down the country. Curry *kapitan* is a splendid dish that is a stock standard among the Peranakans. It includes a slightly longer list of ingredients including shrimp paste, tamarind and makrut lime leaves, which imbue it with an unmistakeable fragrance and depth of flavour.

The cooking process requires first browning the chicken by shallow-frying it to seal and lock in all of the lovely chicken essence. Good things come to those who wait, as they say – or to those who are willing to go that extra mile!

1. Mix the marinade ingredients thoroughly with the chicken. You can do this the night before and leave the meat in the fridge overnight to marinate. However, I usually just do it on the day of cooking and simply leave the marinating chicken for an hour in its bowl on the kitchen counter to give it time to reach room temperature. It means that your cooking time will be reduced later.
2. Blitz the spice paste ingredients into a fine purée.
3. In a medium-sized pot, warm up the oil. Fry the thighs in small batches (each batch should fit comfortably in one layer at the bottom of the pan) over a medium–high heat so they brown properly. They do not need to be cooked through as they will cook further in the gravy later. Put the browned thighs on a plate.
4. Turn the heat down to medium. Deglaze the pan with 100ml (scant ½ cup) of water, then add the spice paste and stir well to mix. Stir-fry until fragrant and the oil separates (which will take a maximum of 10 minutes).
5. Add the seasonings into the pan and stir thoroughly. Return the browned chicken to the pan including any excess oil left on the plate.
6. Bring to the boil then simmer over a low heat, covered, for 20 minutes. Stir every 5 minutes as the sauce can stick, especially towards the end of cooking.

SARAWAK WHITE CHICKEN

6 skinless, bone-in chicken thighs
1 tsp salt
1 tsp Sarawak black peppercorns
1 tsp Sarawak white peppercorns
3 tbsp oil
450g (1lb) tomatoes, cut into eighths
300ml (10½fl oz) water
5 laksa leaf stalks with leaves still attached, or more if you prefer a more aromatic version. If you cannot find laksa leaves, use a small bunch of mint, stalks and all
100ml (scant ½ cup) coconut milk

SPICE PASTE
200g (7oz) onion, roughly chopped
2 garlic cloves
2.5cm (1in) ginger
2 lemongrass stalks, roughly chopped

GARNISH
½ handful of picked laksa leaves or mint leaves
½ handful of freshly picked coriander (cilantro) leaves
1 red onion, quartered then finely sliced into semi-circles
2 red chillies, finely sliced
Juice from ½ lime

I had the pleasure of visiting Sarawak in Borneo for the first time in the summer of 2019. My good friend, the brilliant journalist Dr Anna Sulan Masing, took it upon herself to organize a once-in-a-lifetime trip to the market town of Kapit, three hours upriver from the port city of Sibu.

The highlight of our trip was visiting a tribal Iban longhouse deep in the Borneo jungle, perched right next to the mighty Rajang river. There we were treated to a great many shots of rice wine and a beautiful Iban feast. One of the dishes was *manok pansoh*, chicken cooked in bamboo with aromatics picked by the Iban women from their jungle 'back garden' – simple yet effective flavours. The delicate dish showcased the amazing Sarawak pepper farmed by the Iban. If you can get your hands on some, it has an unforgettable floral fragrance. Otherwise, regular white and black peppercorns will do. Ground pepper can be easily substituted in this recipe, but toasted whole peppercorns will give a far superior end product.

The dish we were served in Kapit came without coconut milk, but I have added some to mine as I enjoy the thicker viscosity it brings. You could very happily leave it out and instead of water, use chicken or vegetable stock (bouillon). I have also added more herbal garnish as I love the fresh tartness it brings – so Sarawakians, this is NOT a *manok pansoh* recipe!

1. Marinate the chicken with salt. You can do this the night before and leave the meat in the fridge overnight to marinate. However, I usually just do it on the day of cooking and simply leave the marinating chicken for an hour in its bowl on the kitchen counter to give it time to reach room temperature. It means that your cooking time will be reduced later.
2. While you're waiting for the chicken to marinate, blitz the spice paste ingredients into a fine purée.
3. Toast the black and white peppercorns in a small frying pan (no oil is needed) over a low heat until fragrant. Grind into a fine powder using a pestle and mortar.
4. In a medium-sized saucepan over a medium heat, warm up the oil and then add the blitzed spice paste and ground pepper powders. Fry until fragrant and the oil separates (which will take a maximum of 10 minutes).
5. Add the chicken, tomatoes, water and stalks of laksa leaf or mint. Bring to the boil and simmer, covered, over a low heat for 25 minutes. Stir every 5 minutes to ensure even cooking. Add the coconut milk for the last 5 minutes of cooking. Taste and add more salt if desired. Remove the stalks of laksa leaf.
6. Garnish with herbs, red onion, chillies and a squeeze of lime juice.

LAMB IN TAMARIND AND GREEN CHILLI

1kg (2lb 4oz) lamb breast,
cut into individual ribs
10 green chillies, roughly
chopped
4 garlic cloves
1 tsp white sugar

MARINADE
2½ tsp salt
1 tbsp ground cumin
1 tbsp ground coriander
1 tsp ground white pepper
1½ tbsp dark brown sugar
2 tbsp tamarind paste

My inspiration for this dish was sambal *kambing goreng*, fried lamb chops with green chillies, which I had years ago at Melur – a Malay restaurant in an Edgware Road basement run by Pak Awie and his family, who used to run Malaysia Hall Canteen in Bayswater. It is one of those dishes that lingers in my memory, it was that good!

This dish is sticky, fiery hot and addictive. I guarantee that once you get a taste of the chilli, garlic and lamb-fat topping, you will totally forget your cutlery and eat with your hands for the rest of the meal. It goes very well with rice or flatbreads of your choice.

You will need to start this recipe several hours in advance or the night before to allow for marinating time.

1. Mix all the marinade ingredients together and then combine with the meat. Cover with cling film (plastic wrap) and refrigerate for at least 4 hours or overnight.
2. Preheat the oven to 170°C/150°C fan/325°F/gas mark 3. Place the lamb pieces on a wire rack set over a baking tin and roast for 90 minutes. Check every 15 minutes, moving pieces that are more coloured away from the heat, and turning them over halfway. The meat should be tender enough to pull away from the bone but not falling off.
3. While the lamb is cooking, finely chop the green chillies and garlic together in a food processor using the pulse mode.
4. Remove the lamb from the oven. Immediately wrap it in foil to keep it moist and let it rest for 20 minutes.
5. While the lamb rests, use a fine metal strainer to pour off the fat from the baking tin into a bowl. You want to reserve the lamb fat, discarding any burnt bits of marinade.
6. Add the lamb fat to a large frying pan over a medium heat. Stir-fry the chilli-garlic mix for 2 minutes. Turn off the heat and add in the sugar. Add the charred lamb ribs to the pan and stir to combine. Be sure to get every last drop of the chilli sauce and oil from the pan onto the lamb when you serve it. Eat immediately.

BRAISED CHICKEN IN BEAN PASTE

BRAISED CHICKEN

7 dried shiitake mushrooms,
soaked in 375ml (13fl oz)
of hot water for at least
30 minutes
200g (7oz) onion, roughly
chopped
10 garlic cloves
3 tbsp oil
375ml (13fl oz) water
8–10 skinless, bone-in
chicken thighs
500g (1lb 2oz) potatoes, cut
into 3cm (1½in) pieces
8 hard-boiled eggs (boil for
7½ minutes, then run
under cold water until
cool, and peel)

SEASONING

200g (7oz) bean paste
60ml (¼ cup) light soy
sauce
2 tbsp dark soy sauce
2 tbsp dark brown sugar
1 tsp ground white pepper
½ tsp salt
1 star anise
1 stick cinnamon

SAMBAL BELACAN

6 red chillies, roughly
chopped into small pieces
10g (1 tsp) shrimp paste,
dry-toasted
½ tsp dark brown sugar
Juice from ½–1 lime
(depending on your taste)

This is another recipe that I have adapted from my mother's collection of frequently cooked dishes. *Pong teh*, as it's called in Malaysia, was always a popular dish whenever she cooked it, especially with my father, as it is a classic Peranakan speciality. It is one of the great Malaysian braises – very straightforward and comforting, and high in umami from salty Chinese bean paste and dried mushrooms. If you have the time and inclination, adding the eggs to the dish will add another welcome dimension.

The searing chilli heat from the sambal *belacan* (fresh chilli sambal with shrimp paste) is a perfect foil to the sweet savouriness of the dish. And of course, plenty of rice to soak up the gravy! The sambal *belacan* will keep well in the fridge for around two weeks. It is a brilliant accompaniment to any dishes that use soy sauce or bean paste as a predominant flavouring, as the heat from the chilli and freshness from the lime juice really perks things up.

You can use lemon juice instead of lime and make sure to remove any pips that fall in. To make the sambal vegan, substitute salt or blitzed *nori* seaweed for the shrimp paste. You can substitute with green chillies or, if you are a masochist, bird's eye chillies!

BRAISED CHICKEN

1. Drain the mushrooms and squeeze well, reserving the soaking liquid. Discard the mushroom stalks and cut in half.

2. While waiting for the mushrooms to rehydrate, blitz the onions and garlic in a food processor until fine.

3. Warm up the oil in a large pan over a medium heat and fry the blitzed onions and garlic, stirring often, until the colour darkens and the oil separates. This should take around 10 minutes.

4. Add to the pan 375ml (13fl oz) water, all the seasoning ingredients and the mushrooms along with their reserved soaking liquid, being careful not to pour in the dirt at the bottom. Stir and bring to the boil.

5. Add the chicken to the pan and bring to the boil again. Then simmer over a low heat for 10 minutes, uncovered. Add the potatoes, bring it back to the boil and simmer over a low heat for 15 minutes, covered. Add the eggs to the pan at the end of the cooking time once the heat has been switched off.

SAMBAL BELACAN

1. Pound everything except the lime juice in a pestle and mortar for a few minutes until a pulpy consistency is achieved. Then add the lime juice and mix. Adjust the seasoning to taste by adding more shrimp paste, sugar and/or lime juice as needed.

2. Serve the braised chicken with the sambal *belacan* and rice.

COCONUT AND LEMONGRASS ROAST CHICKEN

1 whole chicken (around
   1.6kg/3lb 8oz)

SPICE PASTE
4 lemongrass stalks,
   roughly chopped
100g (3½oz) onion, roughly
   chopped
4 garlic cloves
1½ tsp ground turmeric
4 red chillies, roughly
   chopped
14g (1½ tsp) shrimp paste
   (or replace with 2 tbsp
   fish sauce)
1½ tsp salt
2 tbsp white sugar
2 tbsp oil

120ml (½ cup) coconut milk

The inspiration for this comes from an excellent Malay dish called *ayam percik*, where chicken is grilled (broiled) over charcoal flames after being marinated in an irresistible coconut and lemongrass sauce. Malaysian-style Nandos if you like! I was asked to write a simple festive recipe for the *Observer Food Monthly* and thought that this classic Malaysian sauce marinade would work a treat. I chose to use more luxurious duck for my original recipe, but I have converted it to work for chicken which makes it perfect for a Malaysian-inspired Sunday roast. It also works very well simply slathered over some skin-on boneless thighs, left to marinate overnight, and then chucked onto a barbecue! The sauce has a hefty chilli kick, so if you prefer less, simply halve the number of chillies and the amount of sugar.

You will need to start this recipe the night before to allow for marinating time.

1. The day before you want to cook the chicken, prepare the marinade by blitzing the spice paste ingredients into a fine purée. Put the paste into a saucepan and fry it off over a medium heat, stirring constantly for 5 minutes. Now add the coconut milk, bring to the boil and simmer on the lowest heat for another 10 minutes, stirring often. Turn off the heat. If the sauce is a bit lumpy with bits of chilli or lemongrass, use a handheld blender to blitz it further so that it is smooth. Leave to cool.
2. Once the sauce is cool, use half of it to smear all over the chicken, including underneath and inside the cavity, then place it in a large roasting tray and put it in the fridge overnight, uncovered, to let the flavours penetrate. Save half of the sauce to baste the chicken the next day.
3. The next day, take the chicken out of the fridge and let it rest in its roasting tray on the kitchen counter, uncovered, for 2 hours to dry out further and to come to room temperature.
4. While the chicken is coming to room temperature, preheat the oven to 200°C/180°C fan/400°F/gas mark 6 (fan ovens are particularly effective for roasting meats).
5. Cover the chicken with foil and place it in the oven to cook for 30 minutes.
6. Halfway through the cooking time, discard the foil and baste the chicken with the remaining sauce. Roast for a further 30 minutes.
7. At the end of the cooking time, take the tray out of the oven and transfer the chicken to a board to rest for 15 minutes before carving.
8. Spoon any excess sauce left in the roasting tray over the chicken just before you dig in.

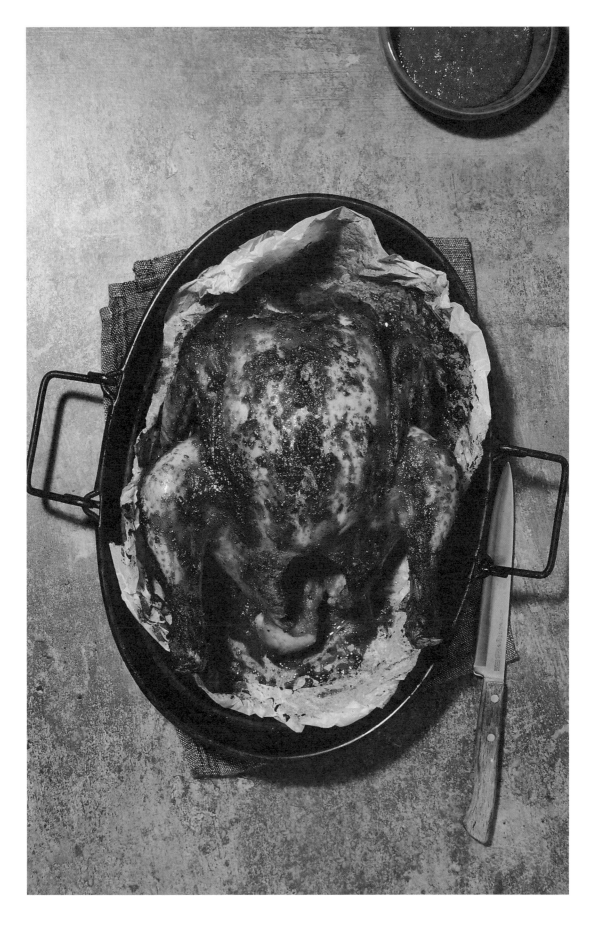

BIRD'S EYE CHILLI CHICKEN

12 green bird's eye chillies (or more if you want some serious eye-watering heat)

1 tbsp ground turmeric

3 tbsp oil

6 skinless, bone-in chicken thighs

1 lemongrass stalk, bruised by pounding lightly with a pestle

200ml (scant 1 cup) coconut milk

300ml (10½fl oz) water

2 makrut lime leaves

1½ tsp salt

1 tamarind skin (optional)

300g (10½oz) sweet potato or potato, cut into chunks (optional)

Stuck for something quick to cook? The first time I cooked this, I was shocked by how little time and preparation this recipe took me. And a Malaysian dish with only a few simple ingredients – very rare!

The Malay name for this dish is *ayam masak lemak cili api* (chicken cooked in fire chillies and coconut milk), which will give you an idea of its flavour profile. Not for the faint hearted! Reduce the number of chillies for milder chilli heat.

It would be delicious with just the basic turmeric, chillies, chicken, coconut milk and lemongrass. The basic recipe doesn't call for potatoes at all, but I think the sweetness from the sweet potatoes helps to cut through the fieriness of the sauce.

1. Blitz the chillies, turmeric and 1 tablespoon of oil into a fine paste using a food processor.

2. Warm up the remaining 2 tablespoons of oil in a large pot over a medium–high heat. Add the chilli paste, chicken and lemongrass. Cook, stirring frequently to turn the chicken, until the outside of the chicken pieces are opaque.

3. Add the coconut milk, water, makrut lime leaves, salt and tamarind skin, if using, and bring to the boil. Simmer, uncovered, for 10 minutes.

4. Add the potatoes and simmer for another 10 minutes, covered. Remove the tamarind skin, if using. Serve with lots of rice.

CHINESE SWEET STICKY RIBS

MARINADE
5cm (2in) ginger, finely
  chopped
4 garlic cloves, finely
  chopped
60ml (¼ cup) hoisin sauce
¼ tsp chilli powder
1 tbsp light soy sauce
1 tsp white sugar
⅛ tsp ground white
  pepper
¼ tsp salt
1 tsp oyster sauce
1 tbsp Shaoxing rice wine
1 tbsp sesame oil

1kg (2lb 4oz) pork ribs
1 tbsp oil
3 spring onions (scallions),
  finely chopped, to garnish
1 red chilli, finely sliced,
  to garnish
2 tbsp sesame seeds,
  toasted in a dry pan until
  fragrant, to garnish

This is my mum's version of barbecue ribs but using store-bought hoisin sauce for its main character. Super easy to put together and one of those rare dishes in this book which uses an oven so you can just walk away and come back later! If you're a fan of *char siu*, you'll love this Chinese take on barbecue. Sweet (but not too sweet), spicy, sticky. The best!

You can use lamb ribs instead for this recipe to make it halal.

1. Mix all of the marinade ingredients together. Use half of it to thoroughly coat the ribs and leave to marinate for at least 1 hour, or preferably overnight.

2. Preheat the oven to 190°C/170°C fan/375°F/gas mark 5. Baste the ribs with 1 tablespoon of oil before laying them out in one layer on a baking sheet lined with foil. Roast for 45 minutes.

3. After 45 minutes, turn the heat down to 170°C/150°C fan/325°F/gas mark 3. Take out the ribs and turn them over. Baste the ribs with the other half of the marinade and then cook for a further 30 minutes.

4. Once the 30 minutes are up, remove the ribs from the baking sheet and leave them to rest for 10 minutes on a large serving plate.

5. Garnish with sesame seeds, spring onions and red chilli.

HAINANESE FIVE-SPICE PORK CHOPS

400g (14oz) pork tenderloin
100ml (scant ½ cup) oil
2 eggs, beaten
160g (5¾oz) plain
(all-purpose) flour
200g (7oz) onion, quartered,
then cut into thin slices
1 star anise
12 garlic cloves, finely
chopped
250ml (generous 1 cup)
water
200g (7oz) frozen peas
2 red chillies, finely sliced,
to garnish
Handful of freshly picked
coriander (cilantro)
leaves or 4 spring onions
(scallions), finely sliced,
to garnish

MARINADE
¼ tsp five-spice
¼ tsp ground cinnamon
⅛ tsp ground white pepper
½ tsp garlic powder
½ tsp white sugar
1 tbsp light soy sauce
1½ tsp sesame oil
1½ tsp Shaoxing rice wine

SAUCE SEASONINGS
60ml (¼ cup) light
soy sauce
1 tbsp dark soy sauce
1 tbsp sesame oil
2 tbsp Shaoxing rice wine
or sherry like Harvey's
½ tsp ground cinnamon
½ tsp five-spice
½ tsp ground white pepper
1 tsp white sugar

My maternal grandfather used to work in the Coliseum, a restaurant in KL dating back to 1921. It is steeped in history and famed for its Hainanese-Western cuisine, originally developed by Hainanese cooks for the British expat community stationed in Malaysia during the colonial era. The cooks were adept at acquiring British and Western culinary skills and preparing Western-style cuisine including soups, steaks and desserts but with a local touch. It is famed for its oxtail soup, cream of mushroom soup, sizzling steaks, caramel custard pudding and Hainanese chicken chop served with chips.

This is one of my mother's brilliant dishes. It centres around pan-fried thin pork chops covered in a fragrant onion and garlic gravy, similar to what was served at the Coliseum.

You can use chicken breast instead for this recipe to make it halal.

1. Thoroughly mix the marinade ingredients together.
2. Slice the pork into 1cm (½in)-rounds, then use a pestle or meat pounder to make them thinner – around 5mm (¼in). Pour over the marinade and leave for at least an hour.
3. Mix all of the sauce seasonings together.
4. Warm up the oil in a wok or large frying pan over a medium heat. The oil is hot enough when a quick, steady stream of bubbles rises around a single wooden chopstick when held upright in the oil.
5. Put the beaten egg in a shallow bowl and the flour in another one. Dredge the slices of pork in the egg and then the flour. Shake off any excess flour.
6. Fry the pork in small, single-layer batches until golden brown – around 2 minutes on each side. Drain on a paper towel after frying to get rid of excess oil.
7. Using the same wok or frying pan, stir-fry the onions with the star anise until the onions start to soften, which should take no more than 90 seconds. Then add the garlic and stir-fry for 1 minute.
8. Add all of the sauce seasonings, water, peas and the leftover flour from dredging the pork. Bring to the boil, stirring frequently to thicken the sauce. The sauce is done as soon as the peas have softened.
9. Arrange the fried pork chops on a large serving platter. Pour over the five-spice gravy and garnish liberally with chillies and coriander or spring onion.

SEAFOOD

GUAN'S SHRIMP, TAMARIND AND BETEL LEAF CURRY

25g (1oz) betel leaves

Leaves picked from 6 laksa leaf stalks

12 makrut lime leaves, stalks removed

70g (2½oz) fresh pineapple, cut into 1cm (½in)-wide bite-sized pieces

150g (5½oz) green beans, hard ends taken off and cut into 5cm (2in) lengths

500ml (2 cups) water

400g (14oz) (peeled weight) raw king prawns (jumbo shrimp) – you can choose to leave the tails on for presentation purposes

SPICE PASTE

1 tsp chilli powder

1 tsp ground turmeric

2 lemongrass stalks, roughly chopped

200g (7oz) onion, roughly chopped

40g (1½oz) galangal, roughly chopped

25g (1 tbsp) shrimp paste

1 tbsp dried shrimp, soaked in hot water for 15 minutes and drained

70ml (2¼fl oz) oil

SEASONINGS

2 tbsp dark brown sugar

3 tbsp tamarind paste

½ tsp salt

My great friend and fellow Malaysian cook, Guan Leong Chua, also comes from a Peranakan background, with a slightly different focus as his family originates from Penang, whereas my father came from Malacca. I had never heard of this dish, *perut ikan*, before he cooked it for me, so was surprised that I instantly fell in love with its powerful, unique flavours.

The Malay name refers to the preserved fish stomach traditionally used for cooking this dish, but Guan cleverly adapted it to use prawns (shrimp). This dish was on our collaboration blue rice *Nasi Kerabu* menu in May 2019 at the restaurant. When I begged Guan for a rough recipe, the presence of lemongrass, shrimp paste, laksa leaves and makrut lime leaves – perennial Peranakan ingredients – explained why I found this dish completely irresistible.

A useful hack is that you can pre-cook the sauce a day or two before you want to eat it, only adding the seafood and fresh herbs just beforehand. It works best with prawns or white fish fillets. You can also use pre-cooked, peeled cocktail/brown shrimp if you don't have raw prawns (shrimp).

1. Finely chop the betel leaves, laksa leaves and makrut lime leaves together using a food processor. Remove the herbs from the food processor and set aside. There is no need to wash the food processor bowl before the next step.

2. Blitz the spice paste ingredients into a fine purée.

3. In a medium saucepan over a medium–low heat, fry off the spice paste for 10 minutes until the oil separates. Stir occasionally.

4. Add the seasonings and stir well to incorporate.

5. Add the pineapple, green beans and water. Bring up to the boil, cover and simmer for 5 minutes over a medium–low heat.

6. Add the prawns and cook for a further 5 minutes, stirring occasionally.

7. Turn off the heat. Add the chopped herbs, stir through and serve immediately.

MUSSELS IN PINEAPPLE CURRY

2 red chillies, roughly
    chopped
100g (3½oz) onion, roughly
    chopped
2 lemongrass stalks,
    roughly chopped
2 garlic cloves
2.5cm (1in) ginger, roughly
    chopped
1½ tsp ground turmeric
25g (1 tbsp) shrimp paste

100g (3½oz) pineapple,
    roughly chopped – if
    using canned, pineapple
    in juice is fine but do not
    use the version in syrup
    as it will be too sweet!
60ml (¼ cup) oil
100ml (scant ½ cup)
    coconut milk
1½ tsp tamarind paste
100ml (scant ½ cup) water
1kg (2lb 4oz) mussels
A few laksa leaves,
    to garnish

The inspiration for this dish is another Peranakan classic – *ikan masak nanas*, fish cooked with coconut and pineapple. You will find chunks of pineapple in the original, but I have chosen to blitz them up for my version to create a velvety curry sauce instead. The tamarind tang and depth from shrimp paste are Nyonya trademarks. A sweet, slightly spicy curry, perfect for summer or midwinter!

You can also replace the mussels with up to 400g (14oz) of prawns (shrimp) or fillets of fish – oily fish like mackerel, salmon or trout would work well. We've served versions using all of these different types of seafood at the restaurant.

1. Blitz the spice paste into a fine purée and then pour it into a container. There is no need to wash the food processor bowl before the next step.
2. Blitz the pineapple into a fine purée.
3. Add oil to a large pan over a medium heat and fry the spice paste until fragrant and the paste has become a darker shade of red.
4. Add the blitzed pineapple, coconut milk, tamarind and water. Bring to the boil and then reduce to a simmer for 5 minutes over a low heat.
5. Add the mussels, turn the heat up to medium, cover and cook for 5 minutes until the shells are open. Garnish with laksa leaves and serve immediately.

TAMARIND PRAWNS

1½–2½ tbsp tamarind
   paste
2 tbsp dark brown sugar
½ tsp salt
3 tbsp oil
100g (3½oz) onion, finely
   sliced
250g (9oz) raw peeled king
   prawns (jumbo shrimp)
   – you can choose to
   leave the tails on for
   presentation purposes
1 red chilli, finely sliced

This is a super-simple dish, like a Malaysian sweet and sour – sweet from the sugar and sour from the tamarind. It is one of my mother's favourite dishes from my grandmother's cooking. It works especially well with prawns (shrimp) as the sauce is a perfect foil to the saline sweetness from the shellfish. It would also work well with small pieces of pan-fried fish, thinly sliced meat or robust vegetables. It's truly versatile and takes no longer than 10 minutes from start to finish if you don't bother with the optional chilli and onion!

Guan Leong Chua served a fantastic version of this at our collaboration events, masterfully done with shell-on prawns – some prefer it made this way so that they're able to suck out the tasty juice from the prawn heads. I prefer this dish cooked with deshelled prawns as I find that none of the delicious sauce is wasted. It really comes down to your personal preference, there is no right or wrong way.

1. Mix the tamarind paste, sugar and salt together (some tamarind pastes are stronger than others so start off with 1½ tablespoons and gradually increase the amount to your taste).
2. Warm up the oil in a non-stick wok or large frying pan over a high heat.
3. Fry the onion until the sides start to turn translucent (this should take no more than 2 minutes).
4. Add the prawns and stir quickly to combine, after which do not move them for 1 minute to let one side properly char.
5. Finally add the tamarind mixture and chillies. Stir-fry for another minute until the prawns are firm. Serve hot.

TURMERIC FRIED FISH

400g (14oz) net weight
  sprats; you can find these
  frozen in East Asian
  supermarkets
100g (3½oz) cornflour
  (cornstarch), to coat
Oil, for frying

MARINADE
2 tsp ground turmeric
1 tsp salt
¼ tsp garlic powder
⅛ tsp chilli powder
⅛ tsp ground white
  pepper

This is a very versatile recipe originating from southern Indian migrants who moved to Malaysia. You can pretty much use any fish of your choice; whole, smaller fish like sprats, as in this recipe, or even small chunks of white fish – but make sure that they are descaled. This recipe also works well with cod's roe and frozen kingfish steaks that are usually found in the freezer section of East Asian supermarkets.

1. Pat the fish dry with paper towels.

2. Mix the marinade well on a shallow plate. Then mix thoroughly with the fish, making sure every part is covered. Leave to marinate in the fridge for at least 30 minutes, or up to an hour.

3. Put the cornflour on another shallow plate and coat the fish before frying.

4. Add enough oil to cover the base of a large frying pan and warm it up over a medium heat. The oil is hot enough when a quick, steady stream of bubbles rises around the end of a single wooden chopstick when held upright in the oil.

5. Fry the fish for 2–3 minutes, turn and then cook through for another 2–3 minutes depending on how thick the fish you are using is. If using fillets, fry the skin side first. There must only be one layer of fish cooking at a time, so if your frying pan is small, you will have to fry in smaller batches.

6. Once the fish is cooked, place it onto a paper towel to absorb any excess oil. Serve hot!

CHINESE-STYLE STEAMED SEABASS

Steamed fish is one of the simplest dishes to execute at home. Traditionally in Chinese households we'll steam fish whole, as a whole fish represents family and unity.

My favourite fish for steaming are seabass, pomfret and lemon sole, in terms of taste and texture. However, you can very easily just steam two fillets of whatever fish you've got! Salmon, hake, trout and cod will all work just as well. I'd save very oily fish like sardines or mackerel for other methods of cooking, as they are better deep-fried, pan-fried, curried or grilled (broiled).

For the traditional wok-steam method you'll need a large wok, a trivet of some kind, and most importantly, a wok lid that closes flush once the plate containing your fish is placed on the trivet. You can buy these trivets in the utensil sections of East Asian supermarkets. Alternatively, you can use a makeshift trivet using a pair of chopsticks, arranged in the shape of a cross, above the waterline in the wok. You will also ideally have an anti-scalding plate gripper to safely remove the hot plate from the trivet later.

Start by adding water to the wok – around 4cm (1½in) from the bottom of the wok – and bring to the boil. The water must be at a rolling boil before you put your fish in.

Typically, a whole fish will be cooked within 8–12 minutes steaming on a medium–low heat, depending on the thickness of the fish. Flat fish like pomfret or lemon sole will be done in 8 minutes. Fillets are much quicker at around 5–8 minutes as there is no bone.

You'll need a glass or porcelain plate or container with a decent lip to securely contain the sauce for the fish. The fish also releases some juice while it steams. A shallow plate will not do, as you risk spilling all of the sauce later, especially if you're using the wok method.

In terms of preparing the fish and its seasoning, I usually rub a bit of oil on the plate before starting, to ensure the fish doesn't stick. If you're using a whole fish, make sure to ask your fishmonger to clean and descale it. Check supermarket fillets of fish, as the majority in the UK have not been descaled for some reason, so you'll have to use a blunt butter knife to descale the fillet yourself.

If you do not have a large enough wok, you can use a simple roasting *en papillote* method in the oven instead. Preheat the oven to 180°C/160°fan/350°F/gas mark 4. Take a piece of parchment paper or foil about 50cm (20in) in length and put it on a baking sheet. Place the fish onto the parchment paper or foil, adding the seasoning on top of the fish. Then fold the sides of the parchment or foil over the head and tail of the fish, bringing the top and bottom pieces together and scrunching them up into a neat parcel. Bake for 20 minutes.

RECIPE CONTINUES PAGE 130

3 dried shiitake mushrooms, soaked in 100ml (scant ½ cup) hot water for at least 30 minutes

1 tbsp sesame oil

2 tbsp soy sauce

80ml (⅓ cup) oil

1 whole seabass (my absolute favourite fish when cooked by steaming for its delicate texture), cleaned and descaled – 600–700g (1lb 5oz–1lb 9oz) is a good size for 2 people

2.5cm (1in) ginger, cut into fine matchsticks

2 spring onions (scallions), finely sliced on the diagonal

1. Drain the mushrooms and squeeze well, keeping the soaking liquid. Discard the stalks and finely slice the mushroom tops.

2. Mix together the sesame oil, soy sauce and reserved mushroom water in a small bowl – be careful not to pour in the dregs of dirt left at the bottom of the mushroom water.

3. Prepare your wok and trivet, as per the instructions in the recipe introduction. Bring 4cm (1½in) of water up to boil.

4. Dip a piece of paper towel into the oil and grease the plate you are using for steaming.

5. Lay your fish on the plate. Pour over the sesame oil and soy sauce mixture. Add the ginger and sliced mushrooms on top.

6. Place your plate onto the trivet in the wok, close the lid and steam for 10 minutes.

7. While the fish is cooking, warm up the oil in a small saucepan until it is smoking.

8. Once the fish is cooked, carefully lift the plate out of the wok. Add the spring onions on top.

9. Finally, pour the hot oil over the spring onions and serve immediately.

Note: Finely cut matchsticks of ginger are excellent with steamed fish. Thickly sliced pieces of ginger would not be pleasant to eat and do not complement the fine texture of steamed fish.

GOLDEN FRAGRANT PRAWNS

500g (1lb 2oz) raw peeled
   king prawns (jumbo
   shrimp) – you can choose
   to leave the tails on for
   presentation purposes
1 tbsp garlic powder
2 tbsp dried shrimp, first
   rehydrated in 100ml
   (scant ½ cup) water then
   drained, reserving the
   water for the sauce
100ml (scant ½ cup) oil

SPICE PASTE
2 tbsp curry leaves
2.5cm (1in) ginger
4 bird's eye chillies (if you
   want it less spicy, use
   1 larger chilli instead)
4 garlic cloves
100g (3½oz) onion, roughly
   chopped

SAUCE
1 tbsp yellow bean sauce
1 tbsp oyster sauce
1 tbsp light soy sauce
1 tbsp dark brown sugar
1 tsp ground black pepper
Reserved water from
   soaking the dried shrimp

Whenever I'm back in Malaysia I always schedule time for dinner at Meng Kee, a restaurant halfway down Jalan Alor, one of the great food streets in Kuala Lumpur's Golden Triangle. Meng Kee has a large menu with over a hundred dishes, from which you would first choose the type of seafood you want to eat, then choose a sauce to go with it. You will also find chargrilled chicken wings and an excellent version of stir-fried butter prawns (shrimp) with egg floss.

This recipe pays homage to their *kam heong* sauce which goes wonderfully well with *lala* sweet little clams. *Kam heong* means 'golden fragrant' because of the many aromatics used: dried shrimp, curry leaves, garlic, yellow bean paste and black pepper.

Don't be deceived by its ugly, dark appearance. Once you've tasted it, you won't be able to stop eating the sauce alone with rice – the prawns in this recipe becomes a bonus!

This recipe can be used with a whole host of different proteins and seafood, such as clams, prawns, thin slices of chicken, pork or beef, and even lots of sturdy veg and/or fried tofu puffs. To make this vegan, replace the oyster sauce with mushroom sauce, and replace the dried shrimp with blitzed up *nori* seaweed and a touch of tomato purée to add more umami.

1. Marinate the prawns with the garlic powder for 30 minutes.
2. Blitz the rehydrated shrimp with 50ml/1½fl oz of the oil into a paste and empty out into a small bowl. Blitz the spice paste ingredients into a fine purée.
3. Heat up the remaining 50ml/1½fl oz oil in a wok on high heat until smoking. Stir-fry the prawns quickly until just cooked (this should take no more than 2 minutes). Empty them onto a container or plate.
4. Using the same wok, turn the heat down to medium and stir-fry the shrimp and oil paste until fragrant, which will take around 1 minute. Then add the spice paste and sauce ingredients. Stir-fry until the oil separates, whichshould take around 10–15 minutes. Taste and adjust the salt/sugar to taste.
5. Finally add the cooked prawns back to the wok. Stir to incorporate and serve immediately.

ASSAM FISH CURRY

60ml (¼ cup) oil
1 tsp black mustard seeds
10 curry leaves (optional but highly recommended)
200g (7oz) onion, halved then cut into fine semi-circles
5cm (2in) ginger, finely chopped
2 garlic cloves, finely chopped
3½ tbsp fish/seafood curry powder mixed with 3 tbsp water. If you don't have curry powder, mix together 1½ tbsp chilli powder (or much less if you prefer!), ¾ tbsp ground coriander, 1½ tsp fennel seeds and ¾ tbsp ground turmeric
2 tbsp tamarind paste
1½ tbsp white sugar
1 tbsp salt
200g (7oz) canned chopped tomatoes or fresh tomatoes, roughly chopped
500ml (2 cups) water
400g (14oz) oily fish such as mackerel, sardines, pilchard, salmon or trout, cut into 50g (1¾oz) chunks
100g (3½oz) okra, tops taken off and sliced in half on the diagonal through the middle
100g (3½oz) aubergine (eggplant), preferably the long, thin Asian kind, cut into bite-sized pieces (optional)

This recipe is an ode to my childhood Sunday lunches with my family after church. A firm family favourite was Indian coffee shops where we would feast on *roti canai* (crispy, flaky flatbreads) and *thosai* (thin, crispy crêpes), served with chutneys.

The *roti canai* usually came with a simple lentil or chicken curry or a sour fish curry with a fierce chilli kick.

Ready-made curry powders are plentiful and widely available at market stalls across Malaysia. If you can get hold of it, the Adabi brand range of curry powders is THE classic Malaysian curry taste.

1. In a medium saucepan, heat up the oil over a medium heat. Fry off the mustard seeds and curry leaves. Keep a lid handy, as the mustard seeds will start to pop so you can use the lid as a barrier between you and them!

2. Add the onion and fry until the edges start to become translucent, which will take around three minutes. Add the ginger and garlic and fry for another minute.

3. Add the curry powder paste and fry off over a medium–low heat until the fragrance and red oil is released. This should take around 3 minutes, stirring frequently.

4. Add the tamarind, sugar, salt, tomatoes and water. You will need to add an extra 100ml (scant ½ cup) of water if using aubergine. Bring to the boil.

5. Then add in fish fillets, okra and the aubergine, if using. Simmer for 10 minutes before turning off the heat.

6. This curry keeps well and will taste even better the next day.

PRAWN SAMBAL

1 tbsp ground turmeric

1½ tsp ground coriander

¾ tsp ground cumin

3 tbsp oil

5cm (2in) ginger, finely chopped

200ml (scant 1 cup) water

1 tsp salt

285g (10oz) Sambal Tumis (page 46)

3 tbsp ketchup

200ml (scant 1 cup) coconut milk

2 lemongrass stalks, cut in half and then bruised by pounding lightly with a pestle

4 makrut lime leaves

⅛ tsp ground white pepper

400g (14oz) raw deshelled prawns (shrimp) – you can choose to leave the tails on for presentation purposes

4 hard-boiled eggs (boil for 7½ minutes, remove from the pan and run under cold water until cool, then peel and slice in half)

½ lemon

1 tomato, thinly sliced

½ cucumber, thinly sliced

My mum made this dish often for our dinners at home. It is redolent with shrimp paste, makrut lime leaf and lemongrass – another very Peranakan dish, which we would all wolf down. The sauce is stupendous and pairs incredibly well with the hard-boiled eggs served on the side. If you're feeling like something fresh to accompany it, you can simply slice some cucumber and tomatoes to complete the meal. No fuss, maximum satisfaction!

This is the closest approximation I have been able to get to my mother's recipe. She freely admits that this dish comes out slightly differently every time she makes it, as she never uses a written recipe and just uses the *agak agak* (roughly meaning 'estimate' in Malay) method. Sometimes, if she is in a hurry, it is also quite possible for her to forget an ingredient or two – she has served a version without coconut milk which is much stronger, but still delicious.

My mum cooks the *agak agak* way which can be frustrating at times as it makes my learning of her dishes difficult! She adds ingredients to the pot or pan without using exact measures. This instinctive method of cooking relies on the cook being able to gauge what is required for a particular dish and on her palate to simply adjust the taste to get the desired result. I have taken the guesswork out of the recipe to make it as foolproof as possible, and it is a good use of any spare sambal *tumis* you have hanging around in your fridge.

Ideally, make the base sauce at least an hour before you want to eat it, as it improves dramatically once it has been allowed to cool down. It is a rare dish in this book that uses lemon juice rather than lime to add some acidity before serving. The tomato and cucumber add a welcome fresh crunch alongside the richness of the sauce.

1. Mix the ground spices with 2 tablespoons of water. In a medium saucepan, warm up the oil over a medium heat then stir-fry the ginger and ground spices for 1 minute.

2. Add the water, salt, sambal *tumis*, ketchup, coconut milk, lemongrass, lime leaves and white pepper to the pan, and bring to the boil over a medium–low heat.

3. Turn off the heat as soon as it comes to the boil and leave for at least an hour for the flavours to fully develop.

4. Just before you want to eat, warm up the sauce to cook the prawns. Once the sauce starts to steam and bubbles appear at the sides, add the prawns and stir-fry over a medium heat for 3 minutes before emptying out into a large serving bowl.

5. Squeeze over the lemon juice before serving with the egg halves, tomato and cucumber slices around the dish.

6. Eat immediately.

VEG-CENTRIC

STUFFED TOFU, AUBERGINE AND CHILLIES

VEGETABLES AND TOFU
1 long, thin Asian aubergine (eggplant)
8 tofu puffs
6 red chillies
1 tbsp cornflour (cornstarch)

FILLING
1 spring onion (scallion), finely chopped
150g (5½oz) prawns, deshelled – see below for vegan alternative
150g (5½oz) minced (ground) pork – replace the prawns and pork with 300g (10½oz) rehydrated soy mince to make it vegan
½ tsp ground white pepper
3 tsp cornflour (cornstarch)
1 tsp sesame oil
½ tsp salt

SEASONINGS
2 tsp cornflour (cornstarch), mixed with 2 tsp water to form a slurry
1½ tbsp oyster sauce – replace with mushroom stir-fry sauce to make it vegan
½ tsp salt
¼ tsp white sugar
1½ tsp light soy sauce
⅛ tsp ground white pepper
1 tsp sesame oil
½ tsp Shaoxing rice wine or white rice vinegar

This dish is known as *yong tau fu* and isn't traditionally vegan, but can easily be converted to be! My mum used to make this often for our dinners, and you can make it as simple or elaborate as you like, in terms of how many ingredients you stuff and what you use to make the filling. The only prerequisite are the tofu puffs, being the namesake of the dish. I really recommend using long, thin Asian aubergine (eggplant) for this dish, as their skins are much thinner and the flesh sweeter than the Middle Eastern type.

You can use pork, prawns (shrimp), firm white fish or a combination of these, minced in a food processor, for the filling. And if you cannot find Asian aubergine or tofu puffs, use a couple of red or yellow (bell) peppers instead. Simply cut in half, remove the seeds and slice each half into square-like quarters to be filled.

To make this dish vegan, rehydrated soy mince would work really well for the filling and simply substitute mushroom stir-fry sauce for oyster sauce.

VEGETABLES AND TOFU
1. Slice the aubergine on the diagonal into 2.5cm (1in) pieces. Then lay each piece cut side down on the chopping board, and slice through the centre horizontally, stopping just after halfway, so that you are able to open it up like a small envelope. Salt the aubergines in a colander sitting in a sink and leave for at least 30 minutes.
2. Slice the tofu puffs almost in half, but not completely, so each opens up like a Pac-Man.
3. Deseed each chilli but leave their tops on for aesthetics. Do this by making a neat incision from top to bottom with a knife, removing the pith and the seeds with a teaspoon.
4. After the aubergines have rested for 30 minutes, squeeze them gently in the colander to drain.

FILLING
1. Using a food processor, mince the spring onion, and then the prawns and pork mince (or soy mince, if using). Add these to the other filling ingredients in a bowl and stir well to combine.
2. Working one by one, dab a bit of cornflour into the centre of each piece of sliced tofu puff and vegetable. Insert a tablespoon of the filling into each piece of tofu, aubergine and chilli. If your chillies are big, you will need to use 2 tablespoons' worth of filling.

RECIPE CONTINUES PAGE 142

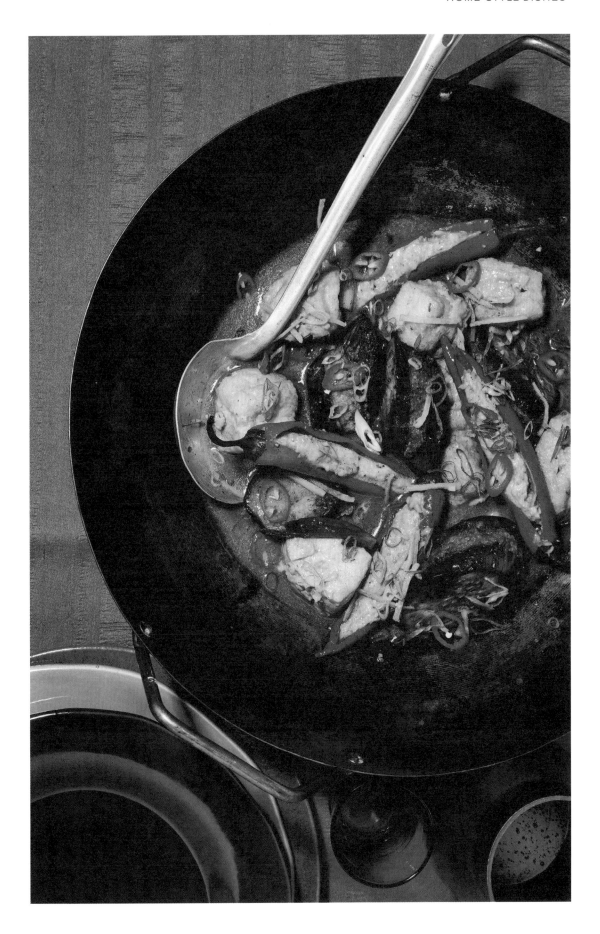

BRAISING SAUCE

80ml (⅓ cup) oil

2.5cm (1in) ginger, cut into fine matchsticks

2 spring onions (scallions), 1 cut into 5cm (2in)-long pieces, 1 finely sliced, to garnish

3 garlic cloves, finely chopped

500ml (2 cups) water

1 red chilli, finely sliced

Finely sliced chillies in soy sauce, to serve (optional)

SEASONINGS AND BRAISING SAUCE

1. Mix together the seasonings in the order that they appear in the list.

2. Warm up the oil in a large frying pan or wok over a medium heat. The oil is hot enough when a quick, steady stream of bubbles rises around a single wooden chopstick when held upright in the oil.

3. Cook the stuffed aubergine first, in two batches, frying gently for 2 minutes on each side. Remove from the pan.

4. Add the 5cm (2in)-long pieces of spring onion to the pan and fry, stirring every now and then, for 1 minute. Add the ginger and stir-fry for 30 seconds, and then the garlic for 10 seconds.

5. Pour in the water and sauce seasonings, and bring the pan to a low simmer. Once the sauce has thickened, add the chillies and tofu puffs (filled-sides up) and simmer for 3 minutes until the filling is cooked. Add the fried aubergine, stirring gently to coat with the sauce.

6. Serve immediately, garnished with sliced spring onions and chilli. Serve with the chillies in soy sauce, if using.

MAMAK INDIAN LENTIL CURRY

SERVES 4

2 tbsp oil
1 tsp black mustard seeds
2 dried chillies
Leaves from a stalk of curry
    leaves (optional but highly
    recommended)
200g (7oz) carrot, sliced into
    2cm (¾in) chunks
1 tbsp tamarind paste
150g (5½oz) canned
    chopped tomatoes or
    fresh tomatoes, finely
    chopped
90g (3¼oz) split red lentils
400ml (1¾ cups) water

SPICE PASTE
100g (3½oz) onion, roughly
    chopped
2 garlic cloves
1 green chilli, roughly
    chopped (use 2 or 3
    chillies if you prefer more
    chilli heat!)
2.5cm (1in) ginger

SEASONING
1 tsp salt
1 tsp ground turmeric
¼ tsp ground cumin
½ tsp garam masala
½ tsp ground coriander
½ tsp fennel seeds

This is my homage to the dhal served at Mamak Indian *roti canai* stalls across Malaysia. Their version is usually quite diluted, but I keep my lentil curry quite strong and thick. Feel free to add more water if you prefer a thinner consistency.

1. Blitz the spice paste ingredients into a fine purée.
2. Heat up the oil in a medium saucepan over a medium heat. Fry off the mustard seeds, dried chillies and curry leaves, if using.
3. Add the spice paste and all of the seasoning ingredients. Fry for 1 minute.
4. Add the carrots, tamarind, tomatoes, lentils and water. Bring to the boil and simmer for around 20 minutes until the lentils are cooked.

VEGETABLES IN COCONUT LEMONGRASS GRAVY

SPICE PASTE

100g (3½oz) onion, roughly
  chopped
2.5cm (1in) ginger, roughly
  chopped
4 garlic cloves
4 red chillies, roughly
  chopped or substitute
  with ¾ tsp chilli powder
14g (1½ tsp) shrimp paste
2 tbsp dried shrimp, soaked
  in 250ml (generous 1 cup)
  hot water for at least
  15 minutes. Drain well
  and reserve the soaking
  water
½ tsp ground turmeric
3 tbsp oil

200ml (scant 1 cup) coconut
  milk
200ml (scant 1 cup) water
1 tsp salt
1 tsp white sugar
1 lemongrass stalk, cut
  in half and bruised by
  pounding lightly with a
  pestle
200g (7oz) carrot, cut into
  3mm x 4cm (⅛ x 1½in)
  batons
500g (1lb 2oz) white
  cabbage, sliced into 1 x
  4cm (½ x 1½in) strips

Sayur masak lemak is ubiquitous around Malaysia, using shrimp paste and dried shrimp to add an irresistible umami saltiness to the natural sweetness of the coconut milk.

This recipe works well with sturdier vegetables, rather than leafy greens. Potatoes and tofu puffs would also be perfect to soak up the fabulous gravy.

You can make this recipe with just shrimp paste or dried shrimp, whichever you have, just increase the quantities slightly to make up for not using both.

To make this recipe vegan, you can replace the shrimp elements using salt to taste or, if you're feeling more adventurous, with a konbu stock (bouillon). Soak 1 piece of konbu in 200ml (scant 1 cup) of cold water for at least 3 hours. Use this konbu water instead of the shrimp soaking water and finely slice the soaked konbu to add to the vegetables in the dish.

1. Blitz the spice paste ingredients into a fine purée.
2. Fry the paste, stirring frequently for 5 minutes until the oil separates – start over a medium heat, then lower it as the spice paste cooks off.
3. Add the coconut milk, reserved shrimp soaking water, the additional 200ml (scant 1 cup) water, salt, sugar and lemongrass. Bring to the boil.
4. Add the carrots and simmer over a low heat for 2 minutes.
5. Add the cabbage, bring back to the boil then simmer over a low heat for 10 minutes until the cabbage starts to become translucent.

MORNING GLORY IN SAMBAL

2 tbsp oil
2 garlic cloves, finely
    chopped
200g (7oz) morning glory,
    cut into 5cm (2in) lengths
3 tbsp Sambal Tumis
    (page 46)
½–1 tsp salt, to taste

This is probably the most popular vegetable stir fry across Malaysia, using our beloved sambal *tumis*. Morning glory (also called water convolvulus or *kangkung*) grows abundantly in Malaysia so is easily available. You could substitute any leafy Chinese greens like kai lan, bok choy, choi sum or even green beans. Just keep the lengths of the vegetable pieces to 5cm (2in) and you will be as right as rain. The sambal *tumis* can be made without shrimp paste if you'd like to make this dish vegan.

1. In a wok or large frying pan, warm up the oil over a high heat and stir-fry the garlic for 20 seconds.
2. Add the morning glory and stir to combine with the garlic.
3. Put a lid on and cook for 3 minutes.
4. Take off the heat and remove the lid. Add the sambal and ½ teaspoon of salt and stir-fry to combine. Taste to check the seasoning and add more salt if required.
5. Serve immediately.

SOY-BRAISED EGG TOFU

SAUCE SEASONING

1 tsp cornflour (cornstarch),
    mixed with 2 tsp water to
    form a slurry
1 tbsp oyster sauce
1 tbsp light soy sauce
1 tbsp dark soy sauce
1½ tsp sesame oil
½ tsp white Sarawak
    peppercorns (if you don't
    have these, whole white
    peppercorns will do),
    ground finely using a
    pestle and mortar
200ml (scant 1 cup) water

2 cylinders (290g/10¼oz)
    egg tofu
100ml (scant ½ cup) oil
2 garlic cloves, finely
    chopped
200g (7oz) minced (ground)
    pork
2 spring onions (scallions),
    finely sliced, to garnish
Small handful of coriander
    (cilantro), chopped, to
    garnish

This is another dish from my trip to Sarawak. On both nights of our stay in Kapit, we ate at a very rustic, family-run restaurant at the edge of town. The mother of the family took orders and served tables with the help of her two young daughters. One daughter had mastered the art of roller skating with plates of food and even bowls of soup! Among all the hustle and bustle of the restaurant a baby slept in a baby basket on top of a spare table, safely tucked away from customers while the grandmother busied herself cooking all of our food in the kitchen located right at the back of the building.

None of us spoke Iban, the most common local tribal dialect and the mother spoke no English. Thankfully I was able to give her our order in basic Malay!

We ordered this wonderfully comforting dish which came with finely sliced wood ear mushrooms. This restaurant also served phenomenal lard-fried thick egg noodles, very similar to the black charred *hokkien mee* you would find in KL. Simple stir-fried greens, a soup and stir-fried butter prawns (shrimp) with egg floss rounded off our meals.

You can make this dish vegetarian by substituting the pork with an equal amount of minced, rehydrated shiitake mushrooms and using mushroom stir-fry sauce instead of oyster sauce.

1. Mix together the ingredients for the sauce seasoning, in the order they appear, in a small measuring jug.
2. Cut through the middle of each cylinder of egg tofu with a sharp knife. The egg tofu will slide out easily. Handle with care, as it is very fragile! Cut into rounds with a thickness of 1.5cm (⅝in).
3. Heat the oil in a large frying pan over a medium heat. Carefully fill the frying pan with the egg tofu rounds. Fry on both sides until golden (around 5 minutes on each side), using a palette knife to turn halfway through. Remove the egg tofu from the pan and drain on a paper towel. Set aside while you cook the sauce.
4. In the same frying pan, add the minced garlic and fry over a high heat for 30 seconds. Add the minced pork and fry for a few minutes until the pork has cooked completely.
5. Add the sauce seasoning, bring to the boil and stir until it achieves the consistency of a light gravy. Turn off the heat and add the fried egg tofu back into the pan, stirring gently to mix through.
6. Serve immediately, garnished with spring onion and coriander.

GREENS WITH GARLIC AND OYSTER SAUCE

1 romaine lettuce (you can use regular lettuce too, or any leafy greens like Chinese or Savoy cabbage, choi sum, bok choy or kangkung/morning glory)
2 tbsp oil
2 garlic cloves, finely chopped
2 tbsp oyster sauce
⅛ tsp ground white pepper
Fried Shallots (page 23)

This is one of the simplest vegetable dishes but it delivers massively on flavour. The steam/fry method leaves you with leaves that have just wilted, yet still have a great crunch to them. It is traditionally served with Pork Herbal Soup (page 86).

My British husband tells me that before meeting me, it had never occurred to him to use lettuce for anything else but salads. He now absolutely loves this dish and has learned to make it himself!

To make this dish vegan, use mushroom stir-fry sauce instead of oyster sauce.

1. Cut the lettuce into large bite-sized pieces.
2. In a wok or large frying pan, over a high heat, warm up the oil then stir-fry the garlic for 20 seconds.
3. Add the lettuce and stir to combine with the garlic. Add a splash of water (about 50ml/1½fl oz) and quickly put a lid on. Cook for 3 minutes.
4. Take off the heat and remove the lid. Add the oyster sauce and white pepper, stirring quickly to combine.
5. Sprinkle with fried shallots and serve immediately.

SAMBAL MAPO TOFU

4 dried shiitake mushrooms,
    soaked in 375ml (13fl oz)
    hot water for at least
    30 minutes
6 garlic cloves
3 tbsp oil
400g (14oz) firm tofu,
    drained and cut into
    1cm (½in) cubes
Handful of freshly picked
    coriander (cilantro) leaves
    and 2 fresh spring onions
    (scallions), finely sliced
    to garnish

SEASONING
1½ tbsp bean paste
1 tbsp tomato purée
3 tbsp Sambal Tumis (page
    46) (this can be made
    with or without shrimp
    paste)
1½ tbsp Lao Gan Ma chilli
    crisp oil (as much of the
    solid bits as possible,
    rather than the oil)
¼–½ teaspoon Sichuan
    peppercorn powder,
    to taste

My love of mapo tofu stems from the first taste of Mission Chinese's eye-wateringly spicy version in New York, and then grew back home in London with Black Axe Mangal's masterful riff with enoki mushrooms and hash browns.

There are, of course, many recipes for mapo tofu, most using minced (ground) pork or beef. I developed this recipe for the restaurant as it combines my favourite numbing, tingly *ma la* Sichuan peppercorn-flavour with my house sambal *tumis* for a Malaysian twist. And I especially wanted to use shiitake mushrooms instead of meat to make it vegan. It became an incredibly popular dish with our vegan customers, as the mushrooms add a deep, meaty flavour. I urge you to make this with the vegan sambal *tumis* if you're having any vegan friends over for dinner as they will be blown away! The additional Sichuan peppercorn powder is optional but gives an extra hit of *ma la*. You could increase it to half or even a whole teaspoon's worth if you're feeling brave.

Lao Gan Ma is an unmistakable brand of chilli oils widely available at East Asian supermarkets. For this recipe, ideally use the chilli crisp version, but the taste won't be very far from the mark if you want to use any of the other variations of Lao Gan Ma that you already have in your store cupboard.

Serve with plenty of rice or, if you're feeling leftfield, this also goes fantastically well as a topping for baked potatoes with lashings of grated Cheddar – an homage to Lee Tiernan's hash-brown version. Delicious!

1. Mince the garlic in a small food processor, then set aside.
2. Remove the mushrooms from the water by hand, squeezing each well, one by one, and reserving the soaking liquid. Discard the mushroom stalks and then mince the mushroom tops in the food processor (no need to clean after the garlic).
3. Combine the seasoning in a small bowl.
4. In a medium saucepan, heat the oil and fry the minced garlic over a medium heat until it begins to turn golden around the edges. Then add the minced mushrooms and stir-fry for 30 seconds.
5. Add the bowl of seasoning mixture and stir-fry for 1 minute, stirring occasionally.
6. Pour in the mushroom water, being careful not to add in any bits of sediment. Bring the sauce to a simmer, then reduce the heat to low and continue to simmer gently for 5 minutes.
7. Bring a pot of well-salted water (it should taste like the sea) to the boil. Blanch the tofu cubes for 1 minute, then drain. Combine the blanched tofu with the braise mixture in the other saucepan.
8. Decant into a dish and top with coriander and spring onions.

SNACKS

We Malaysians are a nation of avid snackers. It is normal for us to eat five or six times a day! Breakfast, a mid-morning snack, lunch, a mid-afternoon snack, dinner, then finally *siu yeh*. *Siu yeh* is the period at night in between dinner and bedtime which one can spend eating and passing time with friends and family. I refer to *siu yeh* as supper. These late-evening delights can either be savoured at local hawker stalls or bought from such hawkers and eaten at home. Of course, there is nothing wrong with going out or buying in a couple of treats for oneself if living alone! These snacks are what I miss the most about Malaysia; being able to pop out at any time of day or night to find something most agreeable when you're feeling peckish.

Portion sizes are much smaller in Malaysia and we can put away many morsels in between meals and for *siu yeh*, like deep-fried bananas in batter, *gado gado* salad (a fresh mixture of vegetables, tofu and egg served with a peanut sauce), *apam balik* (a wonderful pancake with a sweetened peanut filling) or a piece of *kueh* (see below). As a side note, larger dishes like fried noodles, *nasi lemak* or a laksa can also be *siu yeh* but may be shared. We will happily eat any dish or snack whatever the time of day and are not tied, for example, to eating a particular item only for breakfast.

Malaysians also have a sweet tooth, although all of our sweets have a salty or herbal element to them to balance out the sugar. They can generally be broken down into three categories:

1. *Kueh*. Malaysian cakes and cookies (sometimes savoury!) which deserve an entire book just to themselves. These can be delicately fried cookies made from rice flour; carefully steamed cakes made with glutinous rice, coconut milk and palm sugar, fragrant with pandan leaves; or precious banana-leaf-wrapped parcels of rice flavoured with spiced prawn floss or sweetened coconut. These *kueh*, especially those from the Peranakan repertoire, can be colourful, using blue pea flowers for a rich royal-blue tinge or jade green from freshly squeezed pandan essence.

2. Sweet soups. My favourite is *leng chee kang* – flavoured with dried longans (a tropical fruit related to the lychee) and lotus seeds for a bit of bite.

3. Shaved ice desserts like *cendol* and *ais kacang*. Textural and cooling, these are perfect for the unrelenting tropical humidity of Malaysia. *Cendol* combines little strands of fragrant pandan rice flour jelly with shaved ice, palm sugar and salted coconut milk. *Ais kacang* uses shaved ice as a base, onto which red beans, sweetcorn, pieces of translucent palm seeds, peanuts and grass jelly are heaped, then drizzled over with rose syrup and evaporated milk, before finally being topped with a large scoop of vanilla ice cream. A riot of colours and textures! Definitely a firm favourite amongst Malaysians year-round and something really decadent to enjoy during more temperate summers. I haven't included recipes for any such desserts as it is quite difficult to source domestic machines in the UK that shave ice finely and fluffily enough. I have mentioned where to find these in KL and Penang in my travel tips (page 234).

Wandering around morning produce markets (also known as wet markets) and night markets selling clothing/bric-a-brac is a popular pastime. Such is our predilection for snacks that there are always several stalls

selling a good variety at such markets, catering for any hunger pangs or temptations while doing your shopping! Irresistibly moreish curry puffs, stir-fried radish cake, prawn fritters and all sorts of *kueh*, too many to mention, are very popular and usually found at these markets.

Malaysia is a predominantly Muslim society. So, whereas alcohol is often the highlight of gatherings in Western cultures, hospitality in Malaysia tends to focus more on snacks and sweets.

Major festive periods like Lunar New Year and Eid will bring a massive increase to the number of snacks available.

During Lunar New Year, shops will start dedicatedly selling jars and boxes stacked floor to ceiling and filled with a mind-boggling array of intricate biscuits, cookies and filled pastries, with popular traditional Lunar New Year songs blaring throughout, wishing customers a happy and prosperous new year! All of these snacks will be labour intensive and usually cost a fair packet, thus making them worthy gifts.

During Eid you will suddenly find large night markets all across town, where hawkers sell many snacks as well as main meals to make the breaking of fast easier and extra exciting for their Muslim customers.

Open houses are very common during these festive periods, facilitating a nationwide merry-go-round of visits to friends and family.

Not only is it imperative that you have snacks available for any guests who turn up (whether invited or more often unannounced), it is considered good manners for you to bring a gift or two, usually of an edible kind, when reciprocating the visit.

Many of the dishes you'll find in this chapter can be a little labour intensive, for example, the spiral curry puffs, prawn fritters or rose cookies. But the effort is 100 per cent worth it, especially if you aren't able to travel to Malaysia. I promise that these recipes will bring Malaysia to you!

SAVOURY

FENUGREEK CRACKERS AND MAKRUT LIME SALSA

CRACKERS
130g (4½oz) plain
  (all-purpose) flour
3 tbsp finely ground
  semolina
2 tsp sesame seeds,
  toasted in a dry pan until
  fragrant
⅛ tsp chilli powder
¼ tsp ground turmeric
2½ tbsp dried methi
  fenugreek leaves
3 tbsp oil, plus extra for
  deep-frying
1 tsp salt
70ml (2¼fl oz) water

*MAKRUT LIME
LEAF SALSA*
1 red chilli, roughly chopped
40g (1½oz) red onion
10 stalks of fresh coriander
  (cilantro), leaves and all
2 makrut lime leaves, stalks
  removed
¼ tsp salt
½ tsp white sugar
300g (10½oz) tomatoes,
  deseeded and cut into
  1cm (½in) cubes
Juice of 1 lime

When I opened the restaurant, I wanted to create our version of prawn crackers but make them vegan, and so this dish was born. My starting point was Indian *methi puri*, but I added toasted sesame seeds to the dough for my own twist.

I also wanted something fresh to dip the crackers into. I love Mexican salsa for its use of coriander (cilantro) and chillies, which are also commonly found throughout Malaysia. To make the dip even more Malaysian, I introduced finely chopped makrut lime leaves.

These crackers are a dream as they retain their crispness for well over a month in an airtight container, though I am sure that you will have no problem polishing off this whole batch within a couple of days. They're supremely moreish, great with a cold beer, with or without the salsa!

CRACKERS

1. Add the flour, semolina, sesame seeds, chilli powder, ground turmeric, fenugreek leaves, 3 tablespoons of oil and the salt to a large, wide bowl, and mix.

2. Add the water gradually while mixing, adding just enough to bring the dough together. Knead for 5 minutes, then cover and set aside for 10–15 minutes.

3. Divide the dough into 20 equal-sized balls. Cover the balls with a clean, damp dish towel or muslin (cheesecloth) while you are rolling the rest out to prevent them drying out.

4. Roll out each ball into a circle with a diameter of 8–10cm (3–4in), rolling them as thin as possible. Make four or five pricks with a fork on the surface of each circle. Cover again with the damp dish towel or cloth while you wait for your oil to heat up.

5. Heat at least 2.5cm (1in) of oil in a large pan on a medium heat. The oil is hot enough when a quick, steady stream of bubbles rises around a single wooden chopstick when held upright in the oil.

6. Deep-fry three or four crackers at a time until they're light golden brown. They will continue to cook after you take them out of the oil, so don't let them get too dark in the pan! Have a large baking sheet with a wire cooling rack on top of it ready to drain the cooked crackers.

7. Remove the crackers from the oil and place on the wire rack, making sure that they don't overlap. They will crisp up as they cool.

MAKRUT LIME LEAF SALSA

1. Blitz the red chilli, onion, coriander, lime leaf, salt and sugar into a fine paste.

2. Decant into a bowl. Add the tomatoes and lime juice.

3. Taste and adjust the seasoning (salt, sugar and/or lime juice), as necessary.

VEGETABLE FRITTERS

VEGETABLES
110g (3¾oz) carrot, grated
   (shredded)
75g (2½oz) red onion, cut in
   half, then finely sliced into
   semi-circles
110g (3¾oz) beansprouts
125g (4½oz) spring onions
   (scallions), sliced thinly
   on the diagonal

FRITTERS
3½ tbsp rice flour
150g (5½oz) gram flour
1½ tsp salt
⅛ tsp ground white
   pepper
⅛ tsp white sugar
100ml (scant ½ cup)
   water
3 tbsp Ginger Chilli Sauce
   (page 50)
Oil, for deep-frying

Ginger Chilli Sauce (page
   50) or Sambal Tumis
   (page 46), to serve

One of the joys of having the restaurant is being able to give members of my team the opportunity to introduce a new dish to our menu. So long as the dish incorporates a Malaysian element and is easy to execute during service, I am happy! Erin Ward came up with this crowd-pleasing snack based on Indian pakoras, using the fresh vegetables that we had available and also the ginger chilli sauce usually served with Hainanese chicken rice.

The fritters are delicious on their own (because the batter is sufficiently seasoned) but they're also brilliant served with the ginger chilli sauce or sambal *tumis* for extra oomph.

VEGETABLES

1. The most important aspect of this recipe is to make sure that the vegetables are as dry as possible so that they do not dilute the batter later on. Once all of the vegetables have been prepared, mix them together.

FRITTERS

1. Mix the rice and gram flours together.
2. Combine the other dry ingredients into the bowl with the flours and mix with a whisk. Make a well in the centre and slowly add the water and then the ginger chilli sauce, whisking all the while until the batter is smooth.
3. Heat at least 2.5cm (1in) of oil in a large pan on a medium–high heat. The oil is hot enough when a quick, steady stream of bubbles rises around a single wooden chopstick when held upright in the oil.
4. Mix the batter with the shredded vegetables by hand. There should be just enough batter to coat the vegetables and the mixture shouldn't be too wet.
5. Using a tablespoon, spoon the fritter mixture into the hot oil, 1 tablespoon at a time. The mixture may stick to the spoon a bit but simply shake to loosen. Cook for 1–1½ minutes, rotating every so often, until golden brown. Place on a paper towel on top of a large baking sheet to soak up any excess oil.

PRAWN FRITTERS

140g (5oz) plain
(all-purpose) flour
2 tbsp rice flour
1 tbsp cornflour (cornstarch)
¼ tsp bicarbonate of soda
(baking soda)
½ tsp salt
⅛ tsp ground white
pepper
½ tsp white sugar
250ml (generous 1 cup)
water
2 spring onions (scallions),
thinly sliced
Oil, for deep frying
175g (6oz) cooked and
peeled cocktail prawns
(shrimp)
Lingham's jazzed-up sweet
chilli sauce (page 20) or
Tamarind Sambal (page
178), to serve

Prawn (shrimp) fritters are the grown-up sister of prawn crackers. A spiced rice-flour batter is fried into thin, crispy discs before small prawns (shrimp), shells and heads still intact, are dropped into the discs.

There is a stall on Jalan Hang Lekir, just off KL's famous Petaling Street in Chinatown, that sells mountains of these prawn fritters, freshly fried. I used to stop there with my mother after our *wan tan* noodle fix from Koon Kee, right opposite. They are impossible to resist and I cannot think of a better snack than having a few of these dipped into Lingham's (Malaysia's favourite brand of sweet chilli sauce)!

As it is difficult to source small prawns with heads and shells still on in the UK, I have substituted more commonly found cooked cocktail prawns in this recipe. I served these prawn fritters at my *Nasi Kerabu* supper club with Guan in May 2019.

1. Combine the dry ingredients in a bowl and mix with a whisk. Make a well in the centre and slowly add the water, whisking until the batter is smooth. Add the spring onions. Mix well and leave to rest for 30 minutes before using.
2. Heat up at least 2.5cm (1in) of oil for deep-frying in a large pan on a medium–high heat. The oil is hot enough when a quick, steady stream of bubbles rises around a single wooden chopstick when held upright in the oil.
3. Before cooking the first fritter, dip a large metal soup ladle into the oil for a couple of seconds. Using another smaller soup ladle, place about 3 tablespoons' worth of the batter into the heated metal ladle, twirling it to evenly spread the batter around it, then add two prawns on top before submerging the metal ladle into the hot oil. After around 30 seconds, you should be able to loosen the sides of the fritter from the ladle with a small palette knife. Dislodge the whole fritter from the ladle into the oil and flip. Cook for another 30 seconds until both sides are golden brown, then remove and cool on a wire rack.
4. Repeat with the rest of the batter until it's finished.
5. Serve with the lime-boosted sweet chilli sauce or tamarind sambal.

SPICED LENTIL FRITTERS

300g (10½oz) split white urud dal lentils

150g (5½oz) onion, roughly chopped

2 green long thin Indian/bird's eye chillies or 3 large green chillies, roughly chopped

2.5cm (1in) ginger, roughly chopped

A few stalks of coriander (cilantro), roughly chopped

Leaves picked from 3 stalks of curry leaves

2 tsp salt

¼ tsp coarsely ground black pepper

¼ tsp garlic powder

3 tbsp water

Oil, for deep frying

Whenever we used to go to the Mamak Indian restaurant for *roti canai* (flaky flatbread) or *thosai* (Indian crêpes), we would always have *vadai* (spiced savoury doughnuts) on the side. When I first tried *bihari phulki* at Asma Khan's original Darjeeling Express in Kingly Court, I fell in love. It was only later when I was recipe testing for *vadai* that I realized exactly why I loved Asma's *phulki* so much.

In my recipe testing for *vadai*, I inadvertently added too much water, which meant that forming balls that were solid enough to press holes into was impossible. So, I just dropped little balls of the lentil mixture into the hot oil, and lo and behold, the end result was very close to Asma's *phulki*. They are basically a crispier, incredibly moreish version of the puffier, thicker *vadai* of my childhood.

These little crispy pieces of joy would be a great snack to serve at a dinner party, as they are the perfect finger food. And they stay crisp for a couple of hours after frying, so you could make up a batch and still have time to get yourself ready before your guests arrive! Alternatively, they are a nice afternoon snack for the family. You can serve them with a chilli sauce or sambal, but I enjoy them just by themselves, as the aroma from the curry leaves and other spices sings through loud and clear.

You will have to start this recipe at least 3 hours in advance to allow for soaking time.

1. Soak the lentils for at least 3 hours or overnight. Drain well. Blitz the onion, ginger, chillies, coriander, curry leaves, salt, pepper and garlic powder into a fine purée. Then add the drained lentils along with 3 tablespoons of water and blitz into a fine paste in a food processor (if you have a small food processor, you'll have to do this in batches).

2. Warm up 2.5cm (1in) of oil in a large saucepan on a medium–high heat. The oil is hot enough when a quick, steady stream of bubbles rises around a single wooden chopstick when held upright in the oil. Have a large baking sheet with a wire cooling rack on top of it ready to drain the cooked fritters of any excess oil.

3. Scoop up a bit of the lentil mixture with your fingers and then drop small balls of the mixture into the hot oil using your thumb to release each ball. Do not overcrowd the pan as the temperature of the oil will decrease, which will result in your fritters not being as crispy. It doesn't matter if they dissipate a bit when they hit the oil, as the thin tendrils will become nice and crispy. Fry until light brown.

4. Working quickly, turn the fritters in the oil with a slotted spoon so that they cook evenly. Remove them from the oil when they are an even light golden brown, and transfer to the wire cooling rack.

5. Leave to cool slightly before eating as they will crisp up as they cool down.

PRAWN LETTUCE WRAPS

FRESH CHILLI SAMBAL WITH SALTED KRILL

2 tbsp saeu-jeot salted krill, squeezed to drain out the brine

5 red chillies, destalked and roughly chopped

40g (1½oz) red onion, roughly chopped

Juice of ½ lime

WRAPS

Oil, for frying

A few strands of rice vermicelli (optional but highly recommended for textural interest)

Fresh chilli sambal with salted krill

150–175g (5½–6oz) cooked and peeled cocktail prawns (shrimp)

1 baby gem lettuce, leaves separated

4 lychees from a can, drained of the syrup, each lychee cut in half

2 tbsp toasted lightly salted peanuts, pounded in a pestle and mortar into a rough rubble (optional)

Pinch of salt

Freshly picked coriander (cilantro) leaves, to garnish

The inspiration for this dish came from my 2019 Lunar New Year session with my wonderful friend Lap-fai Lee at the restaurant. His delicate *sang choi bao* (lettuce wraps) were filled with prawn (shrimp), lychee, crab and his homemade XO sauce. It reminded me of *cincalok*, which is a fermented krill condiment made only in Malacca. *Cincalok* is impossible to get in the UK and so I hunted down the next best thing – Korean *saeu-jeot*, salted krill that can be found in the chiller or freezer sections of Korean and some East Asian supermarkets.

The resulting sambal is quite fiery, as the chillies have not been cooked off to tame their heat. So, these lettuce wraps are pops of summery joy for any chilli-lover.

You can eat any leftover lychees from this recipe with vanilla ice cream – a very simple dessert for warmer days! You will have to start this recipe at least 3 hours in advance to allow for soaking time.

FRESH CHILLI SAMBAL WITH SALTED KRILL

1. Blitz all the ingredients together in a food processor set on pulse mode so that everything is finely chopped.

WRAPS

1. Heat 4cm (1½in) of oil in a large saucepan. The oil is hot enough when a quick, steady stream of bubbles rises around a single wooden chopstick when held upright in the oil. Drop in the rice vermicelli, if using, and they will magically puff up, becoming a crispy hot mess. Remove them from the oil using a slotted spoon and place on a paper towel to drain any excess oil. Sprinkle lightly with a pinch of salt while still warm. Once cool, break up into smaller strands.

2. Mix the krill sambal with the cooked prawns just before serving, which will keep the sambal as punchy as possible.

3. Choose eight of the larger leaves from the lettuce. To assemble the wraps, take a lettuce leaf and put half a lychee on top of it, cut-side down. Then add a heaped tablespoon of the prawn sambal mixture and a teaspoon of crushed peanuts, if using. Finally, garnish with a nice mound of crispy rice vermicelli for crunch and coriander leaves for freshness.

SARAWAK BUTTER PRAWNS

BUTTER SAUCE

½ tsp white Sarawak peppercorns (if you don't have them, whole white peppercorns will do or if you're lazy just use a teaspoon of ground white pepper. Whole peppercorns will be much more fragrant, though!)

¾ tsp salt

2 garlic cloves

2 tbsp unsalted butter

320ml (1⅓ cups) evaporated milk

2½ tsp cornflour (cornstarch), mixed with 1 tbsp water to form a slurry

1 tsp white sugar

PRAWNS

DRY BATTER

55g (2oz) cornflour (cornstarch)

55g (2oz) gram flour

1½ tsp baking powder

1 tsp salt

125ml (½ cup) fridge-cold soda water

50g (1¾oz) cornflour (cornstarch), for dredging

360–400g (12–14oz), deshelled weight, king prawns (jumbo shrimp)

A few fried curry leaves, to garnish

2 finely sliced red chillies, to garnish

Oil, for frying

This is a dish I associate fondly with Sarawak. Sarawak has a high population of Hakka, Teochew and Fuzhou Chinese from the Fujian province, which makes sense as it is a long boat ride going straight southwards from southern China. The cuisine is not at all chilli spicy, veering towards the sweeter side, and centres around comforting flavours with a fine accent from the famous Sarawak pepper.

Sarawak butter prawns (shrimp) are very different to the stir-fried butter prawns more commonly found in mainland Malaysia, which have tendrils of crispy egg batter. This is a tad sweeter and has a runny sauce, so it is a perfect indulgent starter for four, or a main dish for six, to be eaten with rice as it is quite rich! I had this dish at a Teochew Chinese restaurant in Kuching as part of a multi-course feast arranged by Anna Sulan Masing's family. It was a highlight of that meal for me!

BUTTER SAUCE

1. Toast the peppercorns in a dry pan before grinding them finely with a pestle and mortar. Add the salt and garlic, and grind further into a purée.

2. Melt the butter in a small saucepan over a medium heat. Add the garlic mixture and stir-fry for about 1 minute until fragrant (don't burn the garlic!).

3. Add the evaporated milk, cornflour slurry and sugar. Bring to the boil slowly over a gentle heat, stirring continuously until the consistency reaches a thick sauce – this should take around 5 minutes.

PRAWNS

1. Mix all of the dry batter ingredients in a bowl.

2. Slowly add the cold soda water and whisk until smooth. Leave to rest for 20 minutes before using.

3. Warm up at least 2.5cm (1in) of oil in a medium-sized saucepan over a medium–high heat. The oil is hot enough when a quick, steady stream of bubbles rises around a single wooden chopstick when held upright in the oil.

4. Add the cornflour to a shallow bowl and dredge the prawns through it before coating them in the batter.

5. Fry the prawns in small batches so that there is only ever one layer in the pan. Use a pair of chopsticks or tongs to turn the prawns every 30 seconds to ensure they cook evenly. Remove them from the oil when they are golden and place on a plate lined with a paper towel to drain any excess oil.

6. To serve, pour the sauce over the prawns and garnish with a few fried curry leaves and sliced red chillies.

SPICED TURMERIC PICKLES

MAKES ENOUGH TO FILL A 1 LITRE (34FL OZ) KILNER JAR

200–250g (7–9oz) carrot
200g (7oz) green beans
350–400g (12–14oz) white cabbage
3 tbsp oil
2 tbsp peanuts, dry-toasted and pounded in a pestle and mortar into a rough rubble (optional)

SPICE PASTE
200g (7oz) onion, roughly chopped
3 garlic cloves
25g (1 tbsp) shrimp paste
1½ tsp salt
¾ tbsp ground turmeric
2.5cm (1in) ginger, roughly chopped
3 red chillies, roughly chopped

PICKLING LIQUID
100ml (scant ½ cup) white rice vinegar
50g (1¾oz) white sugar
1 red chilli, finely sliced
2 tbsp sesame seeds, dry-toasted

Achar is a classic Nyonya pickle, widely loved throughout Malaysia. It gives a great tangy crunch to any meal and is a simple way of adding vegetables to your plate when you're in a hurry.

This was on our opening menu at the restaurant as it was a quick and easy snack to send out, being served at room temperature. We left out the shrimp paste and peanuts as these are common allergens and it was then conveniently vegan. Coriander (cilantro) leaves added a pop of freshness.

In this book, I can show you the no-holds-barred version, which is unlike any other pickle you might have had before.

I prefer to start this recipe the day before actually cooking off the pickle to allow more time for the vegetables to dry out. But the end result will still be acceptable if you can't be bothered to wait!

1. If possible, prepare the vegetables the day before you actually cook the *achar*.
2. Cut the carrots into 2.5cm (1in)-long thin batons around 8mm (⅜in) wide. Store the carrots separately as they need longer to cook. Trim the hard tops off the green beans and then cut into 2.5cm (1in)-long batons. Remove the core of the cabbage, then cut into three segments, before cutting across each segment into 1cm (½in)-wide pieces. The green beans and cabbage can be stored together.
3. Refrigerate the vegetables overnight, uncovered, so that they can dry out.
4. On the day you want to cook the *achar*, remove the vegetables from the fridge first so that they come to room temperature while you continue the other preparation for the dish.
5. Blitz the spice paste into a fine purée.
6. Add the blitzed spice paste and oil to a large saucepan. Fry over a medium heat until it dries out and the oil separates, which should take around 10 minutes.
7. Add the peanuts, if using, and all of the pickling liquid ingredients. Stir to combine and bring to the boil.
8. Add the carrots. Stir-fry over a medium heat for 5 minutes, making sure everything is evenly coated with the spice mix.
9. Add the green beans and cabbage and cook for a further 10 minutes. The aim is to cook the outside of the vegetables, but not to cook them through, as you want them to retain their crunch. Turn off the heat immediately (don't leave the vegetables in the pan for long as they will continue cooking if you do) and decant into a clean Kilner jar. Leave at least overnight (or longer) before eating for the flavours to develop.

FRIED SQUID WITH SALTED EGG MAYO

SALTED EGG MAYO
5 salted eggs
180g (6¼oz) mayonnaise
¼ tsp white sugar
¼ tsp chilli powder
2 tbsp water

SQUID

DRY BATTER
55g (2oz) cornflour
    (cornstarch)
55g (2oz) gram flour
1½ tsp baking powder
1 tsp salt

125ml (½ cup) fridge-cold
    soda water
50g (1¾oz) cornflour
    (cornstarch), for dredging
350g (12oz) squid rings
    net weight once defrosted
    (if they've been frozen),
    drained and dried
    thoroughly

A few dried curry leaves,
    to garnish
2 finely sliced red chillies,
    to garnish
Oil, for frying

In SS2, an area in Petaling Jaya, we used to go to this Thai restaurant where we would have incendiary tom yum noodle soup and deep-fried squid in a thick, super-crunchy batter. I love the contrast in textures between the crispy batter and the soft, sweet squid inside.

Another one of my great loves is salted egg yolk – an East Asian favourite. Salted eggs are usually duck eggs that have been left in a strong brine for a month. You can find them raw in East Asian supermarkets. Once boiled, the whites are VERY salty but can be used for simple Chinese vegetable soups or for frying rice instead of using salt. Only the delicious yolks are used in this recipe.

I served this dish at The Sun & 13 Cantons back in 2016. It was always such a crowd-pleaser that I brought it back for my Lunar New Year event at Darjeeling Express in 2018.

SALTED EGG MAYO

1. First make the mayo for dipping the squid into later. Bring a small saucepan of water to the boil, add the salted eggs and simmer for 15 minutes. Lift them out after cooking and immediately place under cold running water to cool. Peel and cut the eggs open, removing the yolks. Blitz the egg yolks with the other ingredients using a handheld stick blender.

SQUID

1. Mix all of the dry batter ingredients in a bowl.
2. Add the cold soda water and whisk briefly until smooth. Let it rest for 20 minutes before using.
3. Add the cornflour to a shallow bowl and dredge the squid rings through it before coating them in batter.
4. Warm up at least 2.5cm (1in) of oil in a medium-sized saucepan over a medium–high heat. The oil is hot enough when a quick, steady stream of bubbles rises around a single wooden chopstick when held upright in the oil.
5. Fry the squid in small batches so that there is only ever one layer in the pan. Use chopsticks or tongs to rotate the squid rings every 30 seconds, ensuring they cook evenly. Remove from the oil when they are golden and place on a paper towel to drain any excess oil.
6. Garnish with a few fried curry leaves and sliced red chillies. Serve immediately with the salted egg mayo on the side for dipping.

MACKEREL 'TACOS'

TAMARIND SAMBAL
100g (3½oz) red chillies,
   roughly chopped
10 garlic cloves
60ml (¼ cup) oil
75g (2½oz) tamarind paste
2 tbsp fish sauce
3 tbsp dark brown sugar
150ml (scant ⅔ cup) water

'TACOS'
100g (3½oz) store-bought
   prawn crackers
4 mackerel fillets – if
   possible ask your
   fishmonger to V-cut the
   fillets to remove the
   small pin bones running
   through the middle
Salt, to taste
Oil, for frying
Tamarind sambal
Cucumber Pickles (page 34)
Large handful of coriander
   (cilantro) leaves

In November 2018 I created this dish for Too Many Chefs at The Drapers Arms, an annual event held for the charity Action Against Hunger. It is great as a starter sharing platter, and would be fabulous done over a barbecue (grill) – the Western equivalent of an outdoors 'wet' kitchen in Malaysia!

I adore this rich, unctuous tamarind sambal, usually found smeared liberally over fried whole fish or grilled (broiled) stingray in banana leaf at Malay *nasi campur* stalls. This sauce is also affectionately known as the 'Three Flavours' – a perfect balance between sweet, sour and proud chilli heat. Yes, our version of sweet and sour!

TAMARIND SAMBAL
1. Blitz the chillies and garlic, and add the oil towards the end of the blitzing. You should end up with a fine, puréed paste.
2. Heat the chilli garlic paste over a medium heat and stir-fry for 10 minutes.
3. Add the tamarind paste, fish sauce, sugar and water, and stir-fry for 15 minutes on a medium–low heat until the oil separates. Stir frequently to prevent the sauce sticking.

'TACOS'
1. Warm up at least 4cm (1½in) of oil in a medium-sized saucepan. The oil is hot enough when a quick, steady stream of bubbles rises around a single wooden chopstick when held upright in the oil. Fry the prawn crackers until they puff up.
2. Dry the mackerel fillets thoroughly with a paper towel. Score the skin to prevent it from curling up when it hits the pan. Lightly season with salt on both sides.
3. Heat a large frying pan with 2 tablespoons of the prawn cracker oil over a medium–high heat. Place the fillets skin-side down. Leave for 3–4 minutes to allow the skin to char. Once you can see the opaque flesh reach nearly halfway up the fillets, flip them and cook for another minute. The skin should be nice and crisp!
4. Serve the fillets whole, for presentation purposes, on large platters with the fried prawn crackers, pickles, sambal and coriander so that everyone can get stuck in making their own 'tacos', breaking off small pieces of mackerel as they wish. Use the prawn crackers like taco shells, adding a teaspoon of tamarind sambal to them, then a small piece of mackerel. Top with cucumber pickles and coriander.

STIR-FRIED RADISH CAKE

*MAKING THE
RADISH CAKE*

700g (1lb 9oz) radish
(mooli), grated (shredded)
200g (7oz) rice flour
250ml (generous 1 cup)
water
½ tsp salt
⅛ tsp ground white
pepper

*FRYING THE RADISH
CAKE (2 SERVINGS)*

300g (10½oz) radish cake
2 tbsp oil
3 garlic cloves, finely
chopped
1 tbsp chai poh preserved
radish (mooli), finely
chopped
2 eggs, beaten
100g (3½oz) beansprouts
6 stalks of Chinese chives,
cut into 2.5cm (1in)
lengths (if you can't get
these, spring onion/
scallion greens are a
good substitute)

SEASONING

1 tbsp oyster sauce
1 tbsp light soy sauce
1 tbsp dark soy sauce
1 tbsp sesame oil
½ tsp white sugar
½ tsp ground white pepper

Sambal Tumis (page 46),
to serve (optional)

When I was growing up, the weekly SS2 *pasar malam* (night market) was the largest in Petaling Jaya, a suburb in Kuala Lumpur. Night markets in Malaysia generally have many stalls selling hot and cold snacks, biscuits, cut fruit, clothes, shoes and kitchen equipment, as well as small trucks offering a wide variety of sweet drinks, *tau fu fa* (silky soybean curd with ginger syrup), *lok lok* (lots of things on sticks for dipping into steaming broths, then finished with hot sauces) and laksa.

For nostalgic reasons, every time I go back to KL, I always make a point to include a stay in Petaling Jaya, just so that I can have a wander around this night market.

My favourite stall at the SS2 weekly *pasar malam* was the carrot-cake man's. I have no idea why it was called carrot cake, when it is not made with carrots, and anyone expecting a traditional Western-style sweet carrot cake will be confused and sorely disappointed!

In fact, the main component of this dish is steamed radish cake. Fried radish cake or *lo bak gou* is a traditional Chinese dish that you will usually find at dim sum – shredded radish and rice flour, cooked low and slow with water until it becomes a paste, then mixed with dried prawns, ham and mushrooms before being steamed. Large blocks are usually then pan-fried until crispy and dipped in chilli oil. When this dish reached Malaysian shores, the fillings were removed to make it cheaper to produce and therefore suitable for a cheap, satisfying meal. The plain radish cake is then cut into much smaller cubes (to increase the surface area exposed to frying) and wok-fried with preserved radish, soy sauce, eggs and Chinese chives.

The carrot-cake man would stir-fry large batches of radish cake on a large, flat hot plate over an impressive gas flame. It has quite similar seasonings to *char kway teow*, another popular Malaysian dish, but the joy of this dish is the addition of preserved radish which gives it a distinctive sweet-salty taste. Preserved radish can be found in small packets in the dried-goods aisle in an East Asian supermarket, usually near the dried mushrooms. They are great in stir fries for a nice salty kick.

This recipe produces quite a lot of radish cake, around 1kg (2lb 4oz). If you are cooking the whole of it for six people on the same day, you'll have to multiply up the ingredients for frying the radish cake and cook in smaller two-person batches for the best *wok hei* – smokiness from the wok.

Alternatively, you can freeze the radish cake once cooked for enjoyment at a later date. It is best to portion the radish cake into 300g (10½oz) portions for two people before freezing. You will just have to squeeze out excess water from the radish cake once defrosted, before you start to fry it.

MAKING THE RADISH CAKE

1. Put the shredded radish into a 20cm (8in) square cake tin.

2. Place the cake tin onto a trivet set over a wok and steam the radish over a medium heat for 30 minutes. Remove the steamed radish from the cake tin and leave to cool in a large bowl. Dry the cake tin with a paper towel and lightly grease it.

3. Mix together the rice flour, water, salt and pepper. Add to the cooled radish and mix thoroughly.

4. Transfer the mixture into the greased cake tin and steam on a trivet set over a wok over a medium heat for 40 minutes.

5. Set aside to cool completely (which will take at least 4 hours or overnight).

FRYING THE RADISH CAKE (2 SERVINGS)

1. Remove the radish cake from the square tin and cut 300g (10½oz) into 1.5cm (⅝in) cubes. Set aside. The remainder can be stored in the fridge or freezer for another day.

2. Mix together the seasoning in a small bowl.

3. Heat the oil in a wok set over a medium–high heat. Add the radish cake cubes and stir-fry until they start to form crusts and become a light golden brown.

4. Push the radish cakes to the sides of the wok, creating space in the centre. Add the garlic and preserved radish/turnip. Continue to stir-fry for 1 minute until it becomes fragrant.

5. Add the seasoning and stir-fry for 1 minute.

6. Add the beaten eggs and stir-fry for 1 minute.

7. Finally, add in the beansprouts and chives, and fry for 2 minutes.

8. Serve immediately alongside the sambal *tumis*, if using.

SAVOURY TARO CAKE

TARO CAKE

3 dried shiitake mushrooms

40g (5 tbsp) dried shrimp

110ml (scant ½ cup) oil
  (ideally the shallot oil
  on page 23 as you will
  need fried shallots for
  the garnish anyway), plus
  extra for greasing

½ tsp white sugar

1 tbsp sesame seeds,
  dry-toasted

3 tbsp Fried Shallots
  (page 23)

50g (1¾oz) onion, finely
  chopped

3 garlic cloves, finely
  chopped

500g (1lb 2oz) taro, diced
  into 5mm (¼in) cubes
  (you must take the time
  to do this, as large,
  uneven chunks will make
  the cake fall apart later
  when you try to cut it)

SEASONING

¾ tsp ground white pepper

¾ tsp five-spice

1 tsp salt

1 tsp white sugar

1 tsp sesame oil

Reserved soaking
  water from shrimp and
  mushrooms

This fantastic snack known as *wu tao ko* can be eaten any time of day. It has many textures and layers of flavour. If eaten in a larger quantity, it can also very easily be a main meal. If ever you're invited to a potluck event, this is the perfect dish to bring, as it is usually served at room temperature. You can make it a day or so in advance, and then simply cube it on the day, before finishing it with the fresh garnishes and drizzling on the chilli sauce.

If you attended my Lunar New Year feast at Darjeeling Express in 2018, you would have tried this then!

Before embarking on this recipe, read it through carefully, noting all of the various vegetable preparation and mixing of ingredients required. It is critical to have all of your *mise en place* ready to go before starting to cook. Frozen taro, found in East Asian supermarkets, works well and is cheaper than buying whole fresh taro in the UK.

1. Soak the dried mushrooms and shrimp in 200ml (scant 1 cup) of hot water for an hour. Squeeze and drain well, reserving the liquid for the seasoning. Discard the mushroom stalks before finely chopping the mushroom tops and the shrimp.

2. Grease the sides of a 20cm (8in) square cake tin with some oil. Line the bottom with baking paper, cut into a square to fit the base of the tin.

3. In a non-stick wok, warm up 3 tablespoons of the oil and fry the mushroom and shrimp mix over a medium heat for 5 minutes. Add ½ teaspoon sugar and stir well to mix. Turn off the heat. Remove 40g (1½oz) of the fried mushroom and shrimp mix and place into a bowl, mixing in the toasted sesame seeds and fried shallots. Set aside for the garnish later.

4. Place the wok back over a medium heat and add the remaining oil to the mushroom and shrimp mix. Add the onions and garlic, stir-frying until fragrant (which should take no longer than 5 minutes).

5. Add the taro cubes as well as all the seasoning ingredients. Stir well to combine, bring to the boil then simmer for 2 minutes, stirring every now and then.

6. Add the dry batter ingredients to the wok. Pour in the water slowly in batches while folding the flour so that it is completely incorporated with the taro mixture and turns into a thick, paste-like consistency. It should come together quite quickly, within 2 minutes. Turn the heat off immediately.

7. Pour the thick batter mixture into the greased square tin and smooth over, flattening and pressing down firmly using a spatula to make sure the cake is even. Steam the cake on a medium–high heat for 30 minutes on a trivet in a wok. Be sure to top up the steam by

BATTER

150g (5½oz) rice flour
1½ tbsp tapioca flour
1 tsp salt
600ml (generous 2½ cups)
  boiling water (use 500ml/
  2 cups if using frozen
  taro, as the tuber takes
  on a lot of water when
  frozen)

GARNISH

100g (3½oz) hoisin sauce
  mixed with 1 tbsp boiling
  water
Lime juice-enhanced
  Lingham's sweet chilli
  sauce (page 20)
2 red chillies, finely sliced
4 spring onions (scallions),
  finely sliced

adding boiling water around the 15-minute mark. To check that the taro cake is properly cooked, stick a skewer into the middle. If it comes out clean, it is done. If not, steam for an additional 5 minutes, or however long it needs, until the skewer comes out clean.

8. While the cake is hot, evenly scatter the reserved mushroom and shrimp mix across the top. Use a tablespoon to press the mix lightly into the cake (it will adhere better while the cake is hot).

9. Let the cake cool for at least 2 hours before using a plastic dough scraper to cut it into approximately 24 small diamonds while still in the tin. Use the dough scraper and a small palette knife to remove the slices from the tin.

10. The slices of taro cake can be warmed up briefly in a microwave before serving (it is more fragrant if served warm) or you can serve it at room temperature. Just before serving, drizzle with the diluted hoisin sauce and Lingham's sauce before sprinkling with chillies and spring onion for a final colourful flourish.

BANANA LEAF-WRAPPED FISHCAKES

400g (14oz) skinless white fish fillets

1 egg

500g (1lb 2oz) banana leaves, wiped down on both sides with a damp cloth regularly rinsed out

10 toothpicks, cut in half

Oil, for greasing

SPICE PASTE

100g (3½oz) onion, roughly chopped

4 makrut lime leaves, stalks removed

½ tsp ground white pepper

½ tsp salt

1 tbsp cornflour (cornstarch)

1 tbsp ground turmeric

1 lemongrass stalk, roughly chopped

1 red chilli, roughly chopped

These fishcakes are a popular snack in Malaysia where they're known as *otak otak*, meaning 'brains', as the texture can be very soft and custard-like when coconut milk is added to the mixture. Banana leaves must be used to wrap them to impart the unmistakable smoky fragrance to the dish. You will find banana leaves in East Asian supermarkets fresh or frozen. I prefer to use fresh banana leaves as I find that they tend to be cleaner.

It is common to see a hawker stall selling only these, much like a satay stall, because it is quite labour-intensive to make these pretty banana-leaf wrapped parcels. *Otak otak* can be eaten by themselves as an excellent snack any time of day, and also go well with rice or as an accompaniment to laksa.

1. First prepare the banana leaves. You will need a ruler! Lay out the banana leaf so that its stem is closest to you. Cut into 20 x 20cm (8 x 8in) squares. You will need 10 squares. Carefully cut away and dispose of the thin stem where necessary, as it will prevent you from folding up the parcel later on.

2. Put the banana-leaf squares in a large container and pour over enough boiling water to cover them. You want to scald them to make them more pliable later on.

3. Dry the fish fillets with a paper towel to get rid of excess moisture before chopping into rough chunks.

4. Blend the ingredients for the spice paste into a fine purée. Add the fish chunks and the egg, and blend until the mixture just about sticks together into a firm paste – don't overwork it.

5. Remove one banana-leaf square from the hot water, shaking to drain any excess water. The parallel lines of the leaf should be running horizontally for ease of folding up the parcel later.

6. Place 1 heaped tablespoon of fish paste towards the bottom half of a banana-leaf square. Roll up the lower end of the leaf around the rice, pressing together tightly before rolling it up to form a fat cylinder. Use the halved toothpicks to secure the ends.

7. Lightly oil both sides of the banana-leaf parcels using a paper towel dipped in a bit of oil. Preheat a large griddle or frying pan over a medium–high heat – turn on your extractor fan or open the window! Place the parcels on the pan and grill for 3 minutes until fragrant and the banana leaf is charred. Alternatively, bake on a wire rack over a baking sheet in an oven preheated to 170°C/150°C fan/325°F/gas mark 3 for 10–15 minutes until the leaves are slightly burned.

8. Discard the banana-leaf wrapper once you've unwrapped a parcel to eat – it is only there to give fragrance during the cooking process.

SPICY PRAWN GLUTINOUS RICE PARCELS

RICE

RICE

300g (10½oz) glutinous rice

200ml (scant 1 cup) coconut
milk

150ml (scant ⅔ cup)
water (include the
reserved soaking water
for the dried shrimp here
for more flavourful rice;
simply top up to make
150ml)

1 tsp salt

1 tsp white sugar

2 pandan leaves, washed
and tied together into a
knot

1 tbsp dried blue pea
flowers (optional)

PRAWN FLOSS

45g (6 tbsp) dried shrimp,
rehydrated in 100ml
(scant ½ cup) hot
water for at least
15 minutes, then drained
well, squeezing out and
reserving the water for
cooking the rice

50g (1¾oz) desiccated
coconut rehydrated
slightly in 3 tbsp water,
left to stand for at least
10 minutes

1 tbsp oil

½ tsp salt

1 tsp white sugar

SPICE PASTE

1 lemongrass stalk, roughly
chopped

40g (1½oz) onion

1 clove garlic

¼ tsp ground turmeric

1 tsp ground coriander

1 tsp ground white pepper

¼ tsp chilli powder (optional
but great if you prefer
more of a kick)

These glutinous rice parcels filled with a spicy prawn (shrimp) floss
are usually found smoking away atop charcoal grills, hence their
Malay name *pulut panggang* (*pulut* means 'glutinous rice', *panggang*
is 'to grill').

Making this popular snack is a fun day's project and best reserved
for special occasions due to its time-consuming nature. It is rather
labour intensive on account of the non-stop stirring of the prawn
floss to prevent burning, steaming the glutinous rice, and cleaning
and trimming the banana leaves. To lighten the load, I recommend
making the prawn floss and preparing the banana leaves a day or
two in advance! You will be richly rewarded though as the cooked
smoky aromatic parcels are so delicious, they will disappear in a
matter of minutes.

I have added streaks of blue to the rice as I find this white and
blue pairing stunningly beautiful, and in keeping with my Peranakan
aesthetic sense! You will have to start this recipe the day before to
soak the glutinous rice overnight.

Pro-tip: You could double or triple the prawn floss quantity and
simply eat it with rice, it is that good! This prawn floss is also used for
tiny fried spring rolls commonly found around Lunar New Year if you
wanted to branch out into making another irresistible Malaysian snack.

RICE

1. Soak the glutinous rice in water overnight and then drain well.

2. Mix the coconut milk, water, salt and sugar together. Place the
glutinous rice into a 20cm (8in) square cake tin or a bamboo steamer
fully lined with baking paper (including its sides). Add the coconut
milk mixture and the pandan leaves and steam on a trivet in a wok for
30 minutes until cooked.

3. While the rice is cooking, soak the blue pea flowers, if using, in
3 tablespoons of hot water for at least 15 minutes, then squeeze dry
to extract the natural blue colouring.

4. After 30 minutes, carefully lift the tin or bamboo steamer out of
the pan. If using, pour in the blue pea flower extract in a rough swirl.
Then, using a plastic rice ladle, roughly mix through the blue colouring
and any coconut cream that has settled on top through the rice. You
should end up with rice beautifully mottled with royal blue.

5. Remove from the heat and set aside until it is cool enough to
handle.

RECIPE CONTINUES PAGE 190

500g (1lb 2oz) banana
   leaves, wiped down on
   both sides with a damp
   cloth regularly rinsed out
1 litre (4⅓ cups) boiling
   water
16 toothpicks, cut in half
Oil, for greasing
Tamarind Sambal (page 178)
   or any other sambal you
   like, to serve

PRAWN FLOSS

1. While the rice is cooking, blend the rehydrated shrimp into a rough mince using a handheld blender. Add the spice paste ingredients to a separate bowl and blend into a fine purée.

2. Stir-fry the rehydrated desiccated coconut in a dry wok or large frying pan until fragrant and light golden brown in colour. This should take around 15–20 minutes – take care to stir frequently to prevent burning. Remove from the pan and set aside to cool.

3. Heat up the oil in a wok set over a medium heat and stir-fry the spice paste until fragrant, which should take no longer than 5 minutes.

4. Add the shrimp and stir-fry for 3 minutes. Add the desiccated coconut, salt and sugar and stir-fry for a final 3 minutes. The end result should be moist, salty, sweet, spicy and deeply moreish.

ASSEMBLING THE PARCELS

1. Next, prepare the banana leaves. You will need a ruler for this exercise! Lay out the banana leaf so that its stem is closest to you. Cut into 12 x 15cm (4½–6in) rectangles, with the longer side measured out and cut from the stemmed side closest to you. You will need 16 rectangles. Carefully cut away and dispose of the thin stem where necessary, as it will prevent you from folding up the parcel later on.

2. Place the banana-leaf rectangles in a large container and pour over enough boiling water to cover them. You want to scald them to make them more pliable later.

3. Remove one banana-leaf rectangle from the hot water, shaking to drain any excess water. Lay it out with the shorter side closer to you. The parallel lines of the leaf should be running horizontally for ease of folding up the parcel later.

4. Spread 1 tablespoon of cooked glutinous rice over the centre of the banana leaf in a thin rectangle around 5cm (2in) wide and 10cm (4in) high, ensuring that the base of the rice rectangle is closer to the bottom edge of the leaf than the top of the rice rectangle is to the top edge of the leaf. Then spread 1 tablespoon of coconut-shrimp filling across the middle of the rice rectangle. Roll up the lower end of the leaf around the rice, pressing together tightly before rolling it up to form a fat cylinder. Use the halved toothpicks to secure the ends.

5. Lightly oil both sides of the banana-leaf parcels using a paper towel dipped in a bit of oil. Heat a large griddle or frying pan over a medium–high heat – be sure to turn on your extractor fan or open the window! Place the parcels on the pan and cook for 3 minutes until fragrant and the banana leaf is charred. Alternatively bake on a wire rack on a baking sheet in an oven preheated to 170°C/150°C fan/325°F/gas mark 3 for about 10–15 minutes until the leaves are slightly burned.

6. Serve warm with your choice of sambal on the side (tamarind sambal goes particularly well with these). Discard the banana leaf wrapper once you've unwrapped a parcel to eat – it is only there to give fragrance during the cooking process.

LAP'S LAMB WONTONS

400g (14oz) Chinese cabbage, cut into quarters, cored and then finely shredded

1½ tsp salt

1½ tsp cumin seeds

1 tsp red Sichuan peppercorns

1 tsp green Sichuan peppercorns

400g (14oz) minced (ground) lamb

1 tsp light soy sauce

200g (7oz) square wonton wrappers

Small handful of picked coriander (cilantro) leaves and/or 2 spring onions (scallions), finely chopped, to garnish

Sambal Tumis (page 46) or any chilli oil, to serve

Note: If you can't find green Sichuan peppercorns, just use 2 tsp red Sichuan peppercorns

These dumplings were the runaway favourite at my Lunar New Year 2019 event with Lap-fai Lee. If you are into the hot, numbing *ma la* flavour, you will love these.

Collaborations over the years have given me immense joy, as I am able to learn so much from my collaborators. Lap served these with his homemade chilli oil full of dried shrimp and a coriander (cilantro) salsa verde. A couple of weeks after our event with Lap, we served rose-shaped dumplings as a special at the restaurant as an homage to Valentine's Day. Our sambal *tumis* is a suitable replacement for Lap's chilli oil, and fresh herbs instead of his salsa verde.

I made a lot of friends at this Lunar New Year event – Yotam Ottolenghi and Helen Goh, Nigel Ng (notoriously known as Uncle Roger), and Louise Hagger, the photographer for this book!

1. Sprinkle 1 teaspoon of salt over the cabbage, toss and let it steep for 30 minutes in a colander.

2. While you're waiting for the cabbage, toast the cumin seeds and Sichuan peppercorns in a dry pan. Then finely grind the toasted spices with a pestle and mortar.

3. Rinse the cabbage, drain and squeeze it VERY well, as excess liquid will ruin the filling.

4. Mix the dried cabbage with the lamb, the remaining ½ teaspoon of salt, soy sauce and ground seasonings.

5. Let the mixture rest in the fridge for an hour before using.

6. Get a small bowl with water ready before you start wrapping the wontons. Place 1 tablespoon of filling in the centre of the wrapper. Dip a finger into water and wet all four edges of the wrapper. Fold over two opposite sides to create a triangle, then wet the left-hand corner before folding it into the middle, doing the same with the right-hand corner. You should end up with what looks like an opened envelope. Repeat with the remaining wonton wrappers and filling.

7. At this stage, you can either cook the wontons or freeze them (which works well). If freezing, lay them flat in one layer on a baking sheet or container and once they've frozen, transfer them into a freezer bag to take up less space. You will be able to cook them straight from frozen whenever you fancy it!

8. To cook them, fill a medium-sized saucepan two-thirds of the way up with water and bring to the boil.

9. Cook the wontons in the boiling water in batches of eight (you're cooking in small batches to make sure they don't stick to each other). Once they float to the top of the water, they are ready to remove with a slotted spoon.

10. Garnish with fresh coriander and/or spring onions, and serve with sambal *tumis* and/or chilli oil.

CRISPY FLAKY FLATBREADS

2 tsp white sugar
½ tsp salt
125ml (½ cup) just-boiled
 water
1 tbsp oil
230g (8½oz) plain
 (all-purpose) flour. If
 you're in the UK, use
 McDougall's plain flour as
 it works consistently with
 this recipe. Otherwise find
 another plain flour with
 a slightly higher protein
 content of 10–11g (¼oz)
 per 100g (3½oz)
¼ tsp baking powder
At least 400ml (1¾ cups) oil,
 for kneading, submersion
 and stretching

I spent years trying to find a good recipe for crispy, flaky *roti canai* like those served by the Mamak stalls my family used to frequent in KL. There are lots of recipes that call for eggs and condensed milk, but I am not convinced that hawkers would choose to use these more expensive ingredients!

There are varying theories on the origins of *roti canai* – some say that they come from Kerala, others that they are from Chennai (both these places are in southern India so are plausible sources).

We are lucky to have Sugendran Gopalai's Roti King in London. I have followed Sugen from when he and his brother Summan were flipping their *roti canai* at a hole in the wall at Oriental City in Colindale, north London, to Kopi Tiam just off Leicester Square, to his first restaurant in Euston and then to his expansion to food-market halls around town.

It took the Covid-19 lockdown for me to crack this recipe, which simply has plain (all-purpose) flour, water and oil as its basis. I had to try making my own *roti* as I could no longer pop to Roti King! My starting point was a Kerala *paratha* recipe sent to me by Krishna Echerlu in my team, that I then adapted. We ate *roti* for every meal for a week while I developed this recipe. I literally danced around my kitchen for a minute when I hit the jackpot!

I hope you enjoy this recipe as much as I do. Being able to whip up a *roti canai* and seeing it puff up in the pan is one of the most glorious feelings I have had the pleasure to experience.

You will need to start this recipe at least 6 hours in advance, or even better, the day before as you can just let the dough rest overnight.

Enjoy your *roti* with a curry with plenty of gravy like Mamak Indian Lentil Curry (page 143) or with a fried egg and Tamarind Sambal (page 178) or Sambal Tumis (page 46) for an excellent breakfast.

1. Add the sugar, salt and hot water to a small measuring jug and stir to dissolve.
2. Pour 1 tablespoon of oil, the flour and baking powder into a large mixing bowl. Add the seasoned water in a slow trickle while stirring with a tablespoon, then bring the components together quickly by hand into a soft, pliable dough. This process should take no longer than a minute – it isn't kneading per se, you literally just want to bring the dough together, rubbing it against the sides of the bowl to incorporate every bit of flour. Do not overwork the dough as this will make it tough later on.
3. Cover the dough with a damp muslin (cheesecloth) or clean dish towel and set aside in the mixing bowl for an hour.

RECIPE CONTINUES PAGE 196

4. Knead using ½ teaspoon of oil until the dough is smooth. Again, this process should take no longer than a minute.

5. Divide into six equal-sized balls. First, roll each ball into a long sausage shape. Then use your right-hand thumb and forefinger to roughly mark the middle of the sausage. Hold one half of the sausage with your left hand and the other with your right. Gently twist and pull the dough in your left hand to narrow the join while using your right-hand thumb and forefinger to work towards forming a smooth cut. Continue to do this until the dough is thin enough to be pulled apart. Then repeat this process to divide each smaller sausage into three portions. Tidy up each portion into a smooth, round ball by rolling it between your hands.

6. Place the six balls into a shallow bowl or container and squish slightly. Then cover with enough oil to completely submerge them. Leave to rest for at least 6 hours. Do not refrigerate.

7. While you are stretching and folding the *roti*, heat a non-stick frying pan or pancake pan over a medium heat. Lightly grease the pan with a piece of paper towel dipped into oil. You only need to do this for the first *roti*.

8. You will need a large, clean and dry surface. Oil the surface well using the oil used during the submersion and place a ball of dough on it. Press down with your palm gently to flatten slightly, and then start rolling it out with a rolling pin, keeping the dough as square as possible, until it is paper thin. Then, starting from the middle, and rotating around the dough as you go, use your fingers to carefully and slowly stretch the dough into as thin a film as possible. You will be able to see where the thicker sections are. The dough should be very thin, diaphanous and almost see-through.

9. Once you have a large, thin square around 40–50cm (16–20in) by 40–50cm (16–20in), sprinkle a bit more of the submersion oil across the entire square. Fold the bottom third upwards and then fold the top third downwards overlapping the first fold, so that you end up with a long rectangle. With every fold, try to trap air in the middle.

10. Then fold the left and then the right sides towards the middle. It is OK if the two sides overlap slightly – you will be left with a small square or rectangle.

11. If you prefer to stretch and fold all the *roti* before starting to cook them one after the other, you can rest the stretched *roti* on a greased plate with baking paper in between each one for up to 30 minutes – any longer and they will start to get too stretchy to handle.

12. To cook, place a *roti* onto the heated pan. After a minute, flip it and cook for another minute. Then flip again and cook for 30 seconds, and flip one last time and cook for a final 30 seconds. Take the cooked *roti* out of the pan onto a chopping board or very flat plate and clap it between your hands to release the crispy layers.

SPIRAL CURRY PUFFS

POTATO CURRY FILLING

POTATO CURRY FILLING

3 tbsp meat curry powder
    (if you don't have this,
    combine ½ tsp ground
    cumin, ½ tsp chilli
    powder, 1 tsp ground
    black pepper, 1 tbsp
    ground coriander and
    1 tbsp ground turmeric)
3 tbsp water
150g (5½oz) onion, roughly
    chopped
4 garlic cloves
3 tbsp curry leaves
    (optional)
5 tbsp oil
750g (1lb 10oz) potatoes,
    diced into small squares
    no larger than 1cm (½in)
    wide
1½ tbsp salt
1 tbsp white sugar
300ml (10½fl oz) water
4 eggs, hardboiled for
    7½ minutes, cooled and
    cut into small pieces

PASTRY

WATER DOUGH

2 eggs, at room temperature
100ml (scant ½ cup) water
400g (14oz) plain
    (all-purpose) flour
¼ tsp salt

OIL DOUGH

200g (7oz) plain
    (all-purpose) flour
150g (5½oz) unsalted butter,
    melted until completely
    liquid
¼ tsp salt

Oil, for deep-frying

In Malaysia you will find curry puffs being sold everywhere as they are one of the nation's favourite snacks. The filling will always be encased in a savoury, crispy pastry. It is the Malaysian samosa or pasty!

But not all curry puffs are created equal – the fried spiral-crust curry puff wins all contests. The spiral-crust pastry is made from combining two doughs in a simple lamination process. You can bake curry puffs, but for me, they must be fried to achieve perfect crispness.

Curried potato and egg are a common curry-puff filling, but you can also use minced (ground) chicken or lamb instead of, or in addition to, potatoes if you like. You will also find curry puffs filled with spicy sardines or sardines fried with onions. I like this potato curry filling the best.

If you are ever in Kuala Lumpur, seek out the famous curry-puff stall in Brickfields which is open during the day. They sell the best curry puffs and fried battered bananas in town!

I highly recommend making the filling the day before you make the doughs and curry puffs themselves to make the process less daunting.

POTATO CURRY FILLING

1. Mix together the curry powder and 4 tablespoons water in a small bowl to form a paste.

2. Blitz the onion, garlic and curry leaves, if using, in a food processor set on pulse mode, so that they end up being finely chopped.

3. Heat the oil in a saucepan or wok over a medium heat. Stir-fry the onion and garlic until the onions have softened, which should take around 3 minutes.

4. Add the curry paste, turn the heat down to medium–low and stir-fry until the oil separates, which will take around 3 minutes.

5. Turn up the heat to medium. Add the diced potatoes, salt and sugar. Stir to mix through. Add the 300ml (10½fl oz) water and bring to the boil. Simmer for around 15 minutes, until the potatoes have softened – take care to stir frequently towards the end as the sauce thickens.

6. Add the eggs and mix through.

7. At the end of the cooking process, there should be a thick, tasty gravy encasing the potatoes. This curry traditionally goes into curry puffs but there is no reason why you couldn't eat with rice, enjoy as a sandwich filling or on top of a baked potato!

 RECIPE CONTINUES PAGE 202

PASTRY

1. Firstly, make the water dough as it needs time to rest.

2. Lightly beat the eggs in a measuring jug, then pour in the water.

3. Combine the flour and salt in a large mixing bowl. Add the egg mixture and mix with a fork to bring together into a scraggly mess. Knead for 5 minutes to form a soft dough.

4. Cover the dough with a damp, clean dish towel and leave aside for at least 30 minutes. Do not refrigerate.

5. Meanwhile, prepare the oil dough. Combine the flour, melted butter and salt in a mixing bowl. Use a spatula to mix well to form a soft dough.

6. Divide the oil dough into 20–22 pieces of 15g (½oz) each.

7. Then, divide the rested water dough into 22 pieces of 25g (1oz) each.

8. Flatten each piece of water dough into a circle. Place a piece of oil dough in the centre.

9. Gather the edges of the water dough to enclose the oil dough. Be sure to wrap the water dough tightly around the oil dough, starting from the bottom. Avoid having any air trapped between the doughs, as this will cause an air-bubble pastry split later on. Repeat the same for the rest of the water and oil dough balls.

10. Cover the combined water and oil dough balls with the damp dish towel to prevent any drying out.

11. On a lightly floured surface, flatten and, using a rolling pin, roll out a combined dough ball into a long, oblong shape – be sure to lightly flour your rolling pin frequently during this whole rolling-out process. Be gentle when rolling out the dough from this point, as you don't want to squeeze out all of the fat that you've so carefully taken the time to layer in.

12. Roll up from one end to the other like a swiss roll.

13. Turn the rolled dough vertically towards you.

14. Flatten out the dough and roll it out again into a long, oblong shape.

15. Roll up like a swiss roll again and put it back under the damp dish towel. Repeat for the rest of the combined dough balls.

16. Cut each small dough swiss roll into equal halves with a sharp knife – concentric circles should be clearly seen on both pieces of the cut dough.

17. Place the cut side of the dough down on a lightly floured surface and flatten with the palm of your hand. Using a rolling pin, roll and shape it into a round, thin skin with concentric circles.

18. Stack the circular dough skins cut-side DOWN under the damp dish towel until you have finished flattening all of the cut dough.

19. Then start filling the curry puffs. Put 1 tablespoon of potato curry filling in the centre of the flattened UNCUT side, which should already be facing up on your stack of skins. Fold and shape into a half-moon and pinch the edges together to seal in the filling. Pleat up the edges.

20. Repeat the same for the rest of the skins, then prepare to deep-fry the curry puffs.

21. Heat 4cm (1½in) of oil in a large saucepan. The oil is hot enough when you can see bubbles form around the end of a wooden chopstick when you hold it upright in the oil. In small batches, gently lower the curry puffs, one at a time, into the hot oil and allow for gentle bubbling over a medium heat. The oil shouldn't be too hot, otherwise you will burn the pastry on the outside leaving it raw in the inside. Only fry one layer of curry puffs at a time so as to not overcrowd the pan.

22. Turn the curry puffs a couple of times to brown evenly.

23. Remove the cooked curry puffs with a pair of tongs as soon as both sides are light golden brown in colour.

24. Drain the crispy curry puffs on a wire cooling rack.

25. Allow to cool slightly, as they will become crispier once cool. These curry puffs are best eaten shortly after deep-frying when the curry puffs are warm but not hot. You do not want to bite into them too soon after coming out of the oil, as the insides will be volcanically hot!

26. If storing, they will keep for a couple of days in an airtight container. To warm and crisp up again, put them into a preheated oven at 170°C/150°C fan/325°F/gas mark 3 for 10 minutes.

Note: The curry puffs are suitable for freezing and then deep-frying just before serving. If freezing, lay them flat in one layer on a baking sheet or in containers. Once they're frozen, you can transfer them to a freezer bag to take up less space. Do not thaw the frozen curry puffs before frying.

PROSPERITY TOSS FISH SALAD

CRISPY CRACKERS
6 fry wonton skins
Oil, for frying

SALAD
300g (10½oz) mild smoked
    salmon
60g (2¼oz) plum sauce
1 tsp sesame oil
1 tbsp water
2 tbsp sesame seeds,
    dry-toasted
¼ tsp five-spice
¼ tsp ground cinnamon
⅛ tsp ground white
    pepper
200g (7oz) radish (mooli),
    grated (shredded)
1 cucumber
1 segment of pomelo
200g (7oz) carrot, grated
    (shredded)
100g (3½oz) red cabbage,
    finely shredded
Large handful of freshly
    picked coriander (cilantro)
    leaves

Yee sang is a very popular Lunar New Year tradition in Malaysia and Singapore. It is a fresh, colourful salad with slivers of raw fish, served with crunchy crackers with an enhanced plum sauce. There are many red/orange components, which for the Chinese is a colour symbolizing good fortune. The different powders can be served in *ang pau* red packets for further symbolism and elaborate presentation.

The idea is that the garnishes and sauce are drizzled onto the salad at the table, just before the eager participants stand up to toss the salad up in the air with chopsticks to mix everything together. It is said that the higher the salad is tossed, the more luck and prosperity is in store for the people around the table!

The amount of each grated (shredded) vegetable is just a rough guide. Feel free to grate as much or as little of each to your liking, and it is totally fine to leave one or two out.

The salad really comes alive with a change of texture from something crispy. If you cannot be bothered to fry wonton skins, I won't judge if you use some good, lightly salted cassava or potato crisps (chips) instead. Just gently use your fingers to crush a couple of handfuls.

Ideally the vegetables should be prepared as close to the salad being served as possible to avoid excess water seeping out. However, you can prepare them a day in advance, but store them in separate containers with folded-over paper towels at the base of each container to soak up excess water.

I have always served this salad at my restaurant and collaboration events around the Lunar New Year period. It was a lot of fun watching guests really get committed to tossing the salad high into the air. Messy for my staff and I cleaning up afterwards, but fun nevertheless.

To celebrate 2021's Lunar New Year albeit in lockdown, I partnered with my friends at Rice Guys on pezu.com to offer a special *yee sang* for nationwide delivery in the UK. Look out for the return of this collaboration in future years!

RECIPE CONTINUES PAGE 206

CRISPY CRACKERS

1. For these crackers, you must use wonton skins that are labelled 'fry' on the packaging. They are more seasoned and crunchier than normal wonton skins when fried. Layer the wonton skins one on top of the other so that their edges are all flush. Then carefully cut them into small rectangles 1cm (½in) wide by 1.5cm (⅝in) long.

2. Warm up at least 2.5cm (1in) of oil in a medium-sized saucepan. The oil is hot enough when a quick, steady stream of bubbles rises around a single chopstick when held upright in the oil. Use a slotted spoon to stir the frying crackers so they cook evenly. Work in small batches, as the wonton skin pieces will bubble up fiercely when they make contact with the hot oil. They are ready when they puff up and are a light gold colour which should only take around 10 seconds. Remove from the oil when they are this colour and place on a paper towel to drain any excess oil. If you're wondering how to use up the rest of the packet of skins, you could fry the remainder to be added like croutons to other salads like the Braised Radish and Shiitake Mushroom Salad (opposite) or use the spare skins to make fried wontons.

SALAD

1. Using your hands, finely shred the salmon.

2. Mix together the plum sauce, sesame oil and water in a small ramekin or saucer.

3. Mix together the five-spice, cinnamon, white pepper and sesame seeds in a small bowl.

4. Gently hand-press the grated radish through a colander to drain off excess water.

5. Cut the cucumber in half lengthways and deseed using a spoon. Grate it then hand-press gently through a colander to drain off excess water.

6. Flake a segment of pomelo into 1 x 1cm (½ x ½in) chunks, making sure that there is no pith.

7. Put the smoked salmon in a small mound in the centre of a large, circular serving plate. Arrange the prepared vegetables in small piles around the salmon, alternating the red/orange-coloured vegetables between the cucumber, pomelo and coriander.

8. Serve the salad with the crispy wonton crackers, plum-sauce mix and dry spices on the side, ready to be sprinkled on top.

9. Toss at the table to mix everything together.

BRAISED RADISH AND SHIITAKE MUSHROOM SALAD

SERVES 2–3

CRISPY CRACKERS
6 fry wonton skins
Oil, for frying

SALAD
4 dried shiitake mushrooms
1 tbsp oil
3 garlic cloves, finely chopped
1 tbsp yellow bean sauce
½ tsp salt
¼ tsp ground white pepper
¼ tsp white sugar
200g (7oz) radish (mooli), grated (shredded)
200g (7oz) carrots, grated (shredded)
Reserved soaking water from the mushrooms
2 lettuce leaves, shredded
3 tbsp hoisin sauce, mixed with a splash of boiled water
2 tbsp lime-juice-enhanced Lingham's (page 20)
2 tbsp lightly salted peanuts, dry-toasted and crushed into a rubble using a pestle and mortar
2 tbsp Fried Shallots (page 23)
3 fry wonton skins (following the method opposite)

In Spring 2017, I was invited by Grace Dent to take part in the inaugural *Evening Standard* 'London Food Month'. At first, I wasn't sure whether to join, as I didn't have a venue. But when my good friend Brídin Allen suggested I use Sourced Market's space on Wigmore Street, Marylebone, I quickly jumped to it. I came up with a 'Memories of Malaysia'-themed menu and sold out eight nights, feeding 320 people!

I try to grab opportunities as soon as they present themselves. From this event, I was named by the *Evening Standard Magazine* as one of the top tastemakers in the London food scene in June 2017.

This dish was inspired by the fresh soft *pohpiah* spring rolls I used to enjoy from hawker stalls as a child. It is labour intensive to make the spring roll skins and you cannot buy them in the UK, so I came up with this just-as-delicious salad instead.

You will need to have the fried wonton skins ready to go, following the instructions in the Prosperity Toss Fish Salad (see opposite).

1. Soak the mushrooms in 200ml (scant 1 cup) of hot water for at least 30 minutes to rehydrate. Drain them, reserving the liquid. Discard the stalks then mince the mushroom tops in a food processor.
2. Warm the oil in a frying pan over a medium heat. Fry the garlic for 30 seconds, then add the blitzed mushrooms and fry for 1 minute until fragrant. Add the bean sauce, salt, white pepper and sugar and fry for 10 seconds.
3. Turn up the heat to high. Add the radish, carrots and the soaking liquid from the mushrooms, and stir to combine. Bring to the boil.
4. Turn the heat down to low and braise for 15 minutes until the vegetables are tender but not soft.
5. To serve, place the braised vegetables on a large plate. Add the shredded lettuce on top and drizzle over the diluted hoisin sauce and Lingham's. Sprinkle over the peanuts, fried shallots and fried wonton skins. Mix at the table and enjoy.

SPICY HERBAL SALAD

1 cucumber
200g (7oz) fresh pineapple, cut into 1cm (½in) chunks
150g (5½oz) red onion, finely sliced
80g (2¾oz) mint leaves, roughly chopped
40g (1½oz) laksa leaves, roughly chopped

DRESSING
3 red chillies, finely chopped
3 makrut lime leaves, stems removed and leaves finely chopped
20g (2 tsp) shrimp paste, dry-toasted
40ml (1½fl oz) lime juice (juice of approximately 2 limes)
2 tbsp light brown soft sugar
½ tsp tamarind paste

Kerabu is an umbrella term in Malay denoting a vibrant salad of vegetables and herbs, dressed with a fiery sambal, shrimp paste and lime to bring everything together. The dressing is spicy, sharp and smells wonderful from all of the herbs. It is a good a way to use up both raw and cooked leftover ingredients.

This is another great recipe that I learnt from Guan. One of the first dishes I tasted from his supper-club cooking was a *kerabu* glass noodle salad with crawfish and wood ear mushrooms.

I have used cucumbers and pineapple for my salad, but in Malaysia you will often find local raw vegetables like four-angled bean and *pucuk paku* fiddlehead fern, as well as fruits like mangoes or jackfruits. Some will also use cooked meat, fish or seafood.

Another beautiful version I've had was in Kapit, Sarawak, featuring tender torch ginger flowers as its main ingredient – it was a fabulous foil to the creamy Sarawak laksa it came with.

Feel free to experiment with different main ingredients while keeping the powerful dressing the same! Just replace the shrimp paste with salt to make it vegan.

1. Cut the cucumbers in half straight through the middle, and then in half again lengthways. Use a spoon to deseed them, then cut into 1cm (½in) chunks.
2. Mix the cucumber, pineapple, red onion and herbs together.
3. Combine the dressing ingredients.
4. Pour the dressing over the prepared salad at least 15 minutes (but no longer than 30 minutes) before serving. Stir to combine. Season with a touch more salt to taste if necessary.

SWEET

COCONUT PANDAN PANCAKES

PANDAN JUICE
8 pandan leaves, cut into
  small chunks
200ml (scant 1 cup) water

COCONUT FILLING
200g (7oz) caramelized dark
  brown palm sugar,
  roughly shaved, or dark
  brown sugar
300ml (10½fl oz) water
200g (7oz) unsweetened
  desiccated coconut
⅛ tsp salt

PANCAKE BATTER
150g (5½oz) plain
  (all-purpose) flour
½ tsp salt
1 large egg
150–170ml (scant ⅔–scant
  ¾ cup) pandan juice
300ml (10½fl oz) coconut
  milk
1 tbsp vegetable oil, plus
  extra for greasing

These pandan pancakes are known as *kueh dadar* or *kueh ketayap*. They probably originated from neighbouring Indonesia and were so delicious that they quickly became a staple throughout Malaysia! Pandan leaves are used to flavour the delicate green pancakes, which are then filled with desiccated coconut steeped in palm sugar. In Malaysia, fresh shredded coconut would be used instead.

I made the mistake of choosing to make these pancakes on *Nadia's Family Feasts* on ITV in November 2019. On the show we had an absolute nightmare trying to flip these pancakes. We lost half of them because we were using the wrong tools!

Since the programme aired, I have discovered that the trick to making these pancakes is that you do not have to flip them because they are so thin! They were a hit as soon as we put them on the menu at the restaurant. To make them a more substantial dessert, I serve them with a simple *crème pâtissière* custard, which is perfect for the winter months.

Both the coconut filling and pancakes can be made a day in advance, and the pandan juice can be made a few hours in advance.

1. To make the pandan juice, blend the pandan leaves and water with a handheld blender or juicer until it becomes a smooth paste. Strain the liquid through muslin (cheesecloth) to extract the juice.
2. To make the coconut filling, dissolve the sugar and salt with the water in a saucepan over a medium heat. Once the sugar and salt have dissolved, add the desiccated coconut and simmer over a low heat, covered, for 12 minutes (or a bit longer if necessary) until almost all of the water has evaporated and the mixture has the consistency of wet sand. Remove the mixture from the pan and set aside to cool.

3. To make the pancake batter, sift the flour and salt into a mixing bowl. Add the egg to the measuring jug containing the pandan juice, and beat to mix. Then add the coconut milk and oil, and stir. Gradually whisk the wet mixture into the dry ingredients to make a smooth batter. Pass the batter through a sieve to make sure there are no lumps. Let it rest for 20 minutes.

4. Heat up a shallow 20cm (8in) non-stick frying pan, or even better, a pancake pan, over a medium–low heat and grease it lightly with oil for the first pancake. Using a small soup ladle, ladle around 3 tablespoons' worth of batter just off-centre into the pan and swirl to coat the base, forming a thin, even pancake of about 15cm (6in) in diameter. When the batter sets and you can see small holes on the top of the pancake or the edges are turning golden brown, loosen the sides and the bottom with a spatula and slide the pancake off onto a plate.

5. Repeat until all the batter is used up, transferring the pancakes from the pan onto a plate with baking paper between each one to avoid them sticking. You should end up with around 15 pancakes. Leave them to cool slightly before filling (they must be filled within a few hours of being cooked – if left overnight, they will dry up, making them impossible to fold).

6. To assemble, turn the pancake over so that the side with the bubbly top is face-down, then put 1½ tablespoons of the coconut mixture just above the bottom edge of the pancake. Fold the pancake over the filling and fold in the sides to enclose the filling before finally rolling it up like a spring roll. Repeat until all pancakes and filling are used up. They can be served cold, or alternatively warmed up in a microwave for a few seconds so that the pandan fragrance is released again.

COCONUT PUDDING WITH SALTED BANANA CARAMEL

400ml (1¾ cup) coconut milk

60g (2¼oz) white sugar

140ml (generous ½ cup) water

2 tbsp cornflour (cornstarch), mixed with 2 tbsp water to form a slurry

¼ tsp salt

A few picked small mint leaves, to garnish

BANANA CARAMEL

2 tbsp unsalted butter

70ml (2¼fl oz) coconut milk

3 tbsp light brown soft sugar

¾ tsp salt

200g (7oz) peeled weight bananas, as ripe as possible, roughly chopped

We did not serve dessert at the restaurant for several months after opening, as we needed to turn seats quickly to cope with the huge number of people who wanted to come in. In the late autumn of 2019, @ClerkenwellboyEC1 asked me if I would be willing to support Cook for Syria for that year's festive season. I used it as the perfect chance for David Griffiths, one of my team, to develop a basic set-pudding recipe that we could use at the restaurant. We used Syrian *muhalabia*, a set-milk pudding similar to a panna cotta, as a starting point but made it vegan with coconut milk. Our Cook for Syria version was topped with pomegranate molasses, peanut brittle and fresh mint.

Since then, we have used different topping combinations at the restaurant to keep the dessert offering fresh and suited to the seasons. The salted banana caramel worked well for winter and reminded me of several banana-centric Malaysian desserts.

I recommend that you start this recipe the day before to allow enough time for the pudding to set.

SET PUDDING

1. You'll need six pretty glasses or ramekins to set these in.

2. Put the coconut milk, sugar and water in a saucepan over a medium heat, stirring occasionally with a whisk to melt the sugar into the liquid. Do not boil.

3. When the coconut milk comes to a gentle steam, whisk in the cornflour slurry.

4. Cook over a medium heat for 10 minutes, whisking and occasionally using a spatula to ensure the mixture isn't sticking to the edges of the pan. If it is thickening very quickly or is catching, turn down and/or take off the heat and whisk vigorously. When the pudding is ready it will look glossy and will thickly coat the back of a spoon.

5. Pour the pudding liquid into a measuring jug, then working quickly, pour it into the glasses. Allow to cool to room temperature before covering in cling film (plastic wrap). Leave to set in the fridge for at least 6 hours or preferably overnight.

BANANA CARAMEL

1. Melt the butter in a small saucepan over a medium–low heat, then add the coconut milk, sugar and salt. Bring to the boil, then add the bananas and simmer for 1 minute, stirring constantly. Turn off the heat and use a handheld blender to blitz the mixture until smooth. Allow to cool to room temperature before using, as it will thicken slightly.

2. To assemble, spoon the caramel over the pudding and garnish with mint leaves.

ROSE COCONUT COOKIES

2 eggs
110g (3¾oz) white sugar
200ml (scant 1 cup) coconut
  milk
125g (4½oz) rice flour
2 tbsp plain (all-purpose)
  flour
¼ tsp salt
1½ tbsp sesame seeds,
  dry-toasted
Oil, for deep frying

These pretty, flower-shaped cookies are known as *kueh rose* or *achu murukku*. They must have originated from southern India as they are also a popular snack at Diwali. I served them at a Lunar New Year event at Asma's Darjeeling Express in February 2018. They are perfect by themselves, or if you wish, with some ice cream.

You will need a brass flower mould, which will either need to be brought back specially from Malaysia or sought out at one of the larger Indian provision stores. It is a worthwhile investment as these cookies are a nice treat for friends at festive seasons year-round, or just for yourself at any time!

1. Add the eggs and sugar to a mixing bowl, followed by the coconut milk, and whisk until the mixture is smooth.
2. Sift together both flours and the salt. Add this flour mixture and the sesame seeds to the wet ingredients in the mixing bowl. Whisk until thoroughly combined.
3. Heat up at least 4cm (1½in) of oil in a large, wide pot or wok set over a medium heat. The oil is hot enough when a quick, steady stream of bubbles rises around a single chopstick when held upright in the oil. Place the brass mould into the oil for about a minute so that it preheats. As you remove the brass mould from the oil, lightly shake off any excess oil.
4. Transfer the mould into the batter and dip just deep enough to cover the sides neatly, leaving the top surface batter-free. You must keep the top surface batter-free otherwise the biscuit will not be able to release from the mould. As the mould gets dipped into the batter, you will hear a sizzling sound as the batter starts adhering to the mould – this is good! Keep still for about 3 seconds to allow the batter to adhere to the mould.
5. Transfer the battered mould into the hot oil, keeping it submerged for about 15 seconds. Do not let the mould touch the bottom of the pot. Lightly shake to free the cookie and leave the mould in the hot oil to preheat for the next one.
6. Let the first cookie fry while you bring in the second cookie (repeating the same steps). Once your second cookie has been released from the mould, lightly hold the mould on top of the first cookie so that the whole cookie gets submerged in the hot oil. Hold it there for another 10–15 seconds (this is to ensure a nice even heat distribution around the cookie, which will result in a light golden brown all round).
7. When the first cookie has turned golden brown, remove it using a flat spatula (using a flat spatula is very important to avoid the cookie losing its shape when you lift it out of the oil). While the spatula is still

RECIPE CONTINUES PAGE 220

in the oil, turn the cookie around so that it is facing upwards on the spatula. Gently let any excess oil drain off the spatula back into the pot before carefully sliding the cookie off onto a wire rack on top of a baking sheet. Leave the mould in the hot oil while doing this.

8. Repeat until all the batter has been used up. When the batter level gets too low for the mould to be fully dipped into, pour it into a smaller bowl before you continue. You will also need a small, fine sieve (strainer) at hand to remove any loose bits of batter from the oil every now and then.

9. Let the cookies cool completely before storing so that they attain ultimate crispness. They are good for 2 weeks stored in an airtight container but they will be gone within a couple of days, I promise you, as they are a bit like Pringles – once you've had one, you won't be able to stop yourself.

SWEET COCONUT RICE CAKE WITH PANDAN CUSTARD

PANDAN ESSENCE
15 pandan leaves, washed, dried and roughly chopped
150ml (scant ⅔ cup) water

RICE
Oil, for greasing
400g (14oz) glutinous rice, soaked in plenty of water overnight
3 pandan leaves, washed, dried and tied into knots
200ml (scant 1 cup) coconut milk
250ml (generous 1 cup) water
1½ tsp salt

PANDAN CUSTARD
Pandan essence (made above)
3½ tbsp cornflour (cornstarch)
1½ tsp plain (all-purpose) flour
5 eggs
180ml (¾ cup) coconut milk
200g (7oz) white sugar
⅛ tsp salt

This is a popular, sweet, glutinous rice-based *kueh* that you will find everywhere in Malaysia. *Seri muka,* or 'pretty face', is so named because the top of the beautifully green pandan custard should be satin smooth and clear of blemishes! This cake is best eaten fresh and not refrigerated. It will keep fine for a day or two at room temperature, assuming that it isn't the height of summer. If you do end up storing it in the fridge, it benefits from being steamed to bring the rice back to life.

Little squares of *seri muka* went down a treat, served as dessert firstly at my Memories of Malaysia Feast in Marylebone as part of the *Evening Standard's* London Food Month over the summer of 2017, spearheaded by Grace Dent. I brought them back as part of my collaboration menu with Asma at Darjeeling Express in the winter of 2019.

PANDAN ESSENCE

1. Blitz the leaves and water with a handheld blender or juicer until it becomes a fine paste, then strain through a muslin (cheesecloth) to extract the essence.

RICE

1. Line a 20cm (8in) square cake tin with baking paper and grease with oil.
2. Pour the rice, coconut milk, water and salt into the tin. Place the three knotted pandan leaves on top and steam on a trivet in a wok or in a large bamboo steamer on a medium heat for 20 minutes. Remove the pandan leaves and stir the rice before steaming for a further 10 minutes.

PANDAN CUSTARD

1. While the rice is cooking, whisk all the custard ingredients together and then pass through a fine sieve (strainer) into a heatproof bowl, to ensure there are no lumps.
2. Place the bowl over a simmering pan of water over a medium–low heat. Stir slowly and constantly with a spatula or wooden spoon until the custard begins to coat it like a thick gravy. This should take a maximum of 25 minutes. Watch the custard carefully as it will thicken suddenly – you must pull it off the heat as soon as it does to avoid any lumps forming!
3. Make sure that the rice is hot and properly cooked before the next step.

RECIPE CONTINUES PAGE 224

4. Pat the rice down firmly to make it as flat and even as possible.

5. Pour the thickened custard onto the rice (which is still in the cake tin).

6. If using a wok to steam the cake, cover the cake tin with foil. However, if using a large bamboo steamer (which won't drip), you don't have to cover the cake tin with foil. Dripping water will cause unsightly pock marks on the surface of the custard, meaning that the cake will no longer be 'pretty', as its Malay name suggests.

7. Make sure to refill your wok with hot water to prevent it boiling dry during the next step.

8. Steam for 25 minutes on a medium heat, or longer, until the middle is set and there is no wobble at all.

9. Cool for at least 4 hours.

10. Carefully remove the cake from the tin and place on a large chopping board. Have a container full of hot water on the side before you embark on cutting up the cake. Using a sharp chef's knife, cut the cake into small rectangles. After every cut, dip the knife into the hot water and wipe clean with a paper towel (warming and cleaning the knife between cuts will give you nice clean lines when cutting the cake).

MAKES AROUND 15

MALAYSIAN CRISPY PANCAKES

BATTER
170g (6oz) plain
(all-purpose) flour
100g (3½oz) rice flour
3 tbsp cornflour (cornstarch)
2 tsp baking powder
½ tsp salt
150g (5½oz) white sugar
2 eggs
250ml (generous 1 cup)
fridge-cold water
1 tsp vanilla extract
(optional)

FILLING
200g (7oz) lightly salted
peanuts, dry-toasted
120g (4¼oz) white sugar
120g (4¼oz) unsalted butter,
melted
250g (9oz) canned creamed
sweetcorn

Hawkers selling *apam balik* are usually found at night markets and use specially made integrated pans to make cooking them more efficient and quick.

This recipe uses my favourite filling – butter, peanuts, sugar and canned creamed sweetcorn. Eastern desserts frequently use savoury aspects and ingredients like sweetcorn, red beans and sweet potato. We also have a predilection for peanuts for their crunch and saltiness. You can use many other fillings in this recipe like chocolate spread and/or bananas, and just omit the sweetcorn.

You will need to start this recipe at least 3 hours in advance, or the day before, to allow enough time for the batter to rest.

1. To make the pancake batter, place all the dry ingredients in a bowl and give it a quick mix. Add the eggs, water and vanilla, if using, and whisk until smooth and lump-free. Cover it with cling film (plastic wrap) and stick it in the fridge for 3 hours (or overnight).
2. For the filling, pulse the nuts and sugar in a food processor and blitz until it becomes a fine rubble (but not too fine that it becomes powdery).
3. Heat up a 20cm (8in) shallow non-stick frying pan or even better, a pancake pan, over a medium–low heat.
4. Before frying each pancake, add a dab of melted butter using a piece of paper towel to grease the pan thoroughly.
5. Using a small soup ladle, ladle 3 tablespoons' worth of batter just off-centre in the pan and swirl to coat the base, to form a thin pancake. Use the back of the ladle if necessary to make sure the batter evenly covers the entire surface, as thinly as possible. It helps to move the pan off the heat to do this, and then move it back onto the heat once you have spread the batter out.
6. Once bubbles have formed over the entire surface of the pancake, sprinkle the peanut filling over the whole pancake. Drizzle 1 tablespoon of melted butter over one half and roughly dollop 1 tablespoon of creamed corn on the other half.
7. Cook until the bottom and sides of the pancake are golden brown. It is ready when the sides of the pancake are clearly peeling away from the pan.
8. Using a palette knife, flip one side of the pancake over the other to fold in half and remove from the pan to cool on a wire rack. Leave to rest for at least 3 minutes before serving as it will become crispy once cooled. If you only have one wire rack, you will need to pause for a few minutes once it is full of cooked pancakes to allow them to cool properly before moving them off into another container to make space for more cooked pancakes.

TARO AND SWEET POTATO SWEET SOUP

GLUTINOUS RICE JELLIES

150g (5½oz) glutinous rice flour (raw NOT cooked)

6 tbsp cornflour (cornstarch)

Natural blue colouring:
5g (2 tbsp) blue pea flowers, soaked in 3 tbsp boiling water for at least 15 minutes, before squeezing out the blue extract. You will need 50ml (1½fl oz) blue extract. If you are slightly short after squeezing out the flowers, then top up with water as necessary

Natural red colouring:
Blitz and strain 100g (3½oz) cooked beetroot (NOT the kind cooked in vinegar!) so that you end up with at least 3 tbsp of liquid. You will need 50ml (1½fl oz) red extract. If you are slightly short after straining the beetroot, then top up with water as necessary

Natural green colouring:
5 pandan leaves, roughly chopped and mixed with 100ml (scant ½ cup) water before blitzing with a handheld blender or juicer into a fine paste. Strain through muslin (cheesecloth) to squeeze out the green extract. You will only need 50ml (1½fl oz) green extract

Alternatively, to save time, use ½ teaspoon of each of three different store-bought artificial food colourings

This is another of our classic sweet-savoury desserts, known as *bubur cha cha*. We love our sweet soups in Malaysia, due to the strong Chinese influence, and also because they are so refreshing when served cold in our tropical climate.

The glutinous rice jellies cement the textural pleasure of *bubur cha cha*, adding a bouncy 'QQ' element to the denser bits of taro and sweet potatoes. Coconut milk fragranced with pandan leaves brings everything together in this wonderful concoction.

I put it on our menu at our pop-up at The Sun & 13 Cantons in Soho. It pained me that it didn't sell as much as I had hoped. Malaysians loved the nostalgic taste of home, but I think others found the texture problematic and couldn't get their heads around eating tubers for dessert. This is the perfect way to eat sweet potato in my view, and if you are a fan of bubble tea, I think you will enjoy this more nutritious dessert.

Making the glutinous rice jellies is great fun, much like playing with Play-Doh! You can, of course, use commercially available food colourings, or if you're feeling more industrious, extract natural colourings from scratch as I have done here. This recipe uses three different colours for the jellies but can be massively simplified if you use just one colour for the whole 150g (5½oz) of glutinous rice flour.

I hope that you will enjoy my mother's recipe as much as I do. My mother uses tapioca flour, in line with more traditional recipes which have a denser bite. I have used glutinous rice flour as I prefer them with a more delicate, chewy texture.

GLUTINOUS RICE JELLIES

1. To make three colours of jellies, divide the glutinous rice flour into three batches of 50g (1¾oz).

2. Place 50g (1¾oz) of glutinous rice flour into a small mixing bowl. Warm up the blue extract in the microwave for 40 seconds or so, until it is steaming. Pour the steaming blue liquid into the flour and mix with a spoon, before using a gloved hand to bring it together into a smooth, slightly tacky dough. It should not stick to the sides of the bowl and should come away easily from your hand. Roll into a neat ball and store in a covered container, to prevent it from drying out, while you're making the other colours.

3. Make the red and green jellies using this same method.

RECIPE CONTINUES PAGE 230

SOUP

200g (7oz) taro (fresh or
  frozen), cut into 1–2cm
  (½–¾in) pieces
2 pandan leaves, washed,
  dried and then tied into
  knots
175g (6oz) white sugar
½ tsp salt
1.25 litres (5½ cups) water
300g (10½oz) sweet potato,
  cut into 1–2cm (½–¾in)
  pieces
200ml (scant 1 cup) coconut
  milk

4. Sprinkle ½ tablespoon of cornflour on a clean kitchen counter and roll one coloured dough out evenly until it is 2–3mm (¹⁄₁₆–⅛in) thick. Sprinkle another ½ tablespoon of cornflour over the top of the dough before cutting it into small diamond shapes. Store the jellies in a covered container mixed with 1 tablespoon of cornflour before using them, to prevent them from drying out/sticking together. Repeat with the other two doughs.

5. Alternatively, to make just one colour of jellies using store-bought food colouring, place 150g (5½oz) glutinous rice flour in a large mixing bowl. Mix in 1 teaspoon of food colouring into 150ml (scant ⅔ cup) of just-boiled water. Slowly pour this coloured water into the flour and using a spoon or chopstick, mix until well incorporated. Use a gloved hand to bring the dough together and knead well to evenly distribute the colour into the dough. Divide the dough into three balls – you are still dividing the dough into three pieces even though there is just one colour to make cutting out the small diamond shapes easier to manage later on. Sprinkle ½ tablespoon of cornflour on a clean kitchen counter and roll a ball of dough out evenly until it is 2–3mm (¹⁄₁₆–⅛in) thick. Sprinkle another ½ tablespoon of cornflour over the top of the dough before cutting it into small diamond shapes. Store the jellies in a covered container mixed with 1 tablespoon of cornflour before using them to prevent them from drying out/sticking together. Repeat with the remaining two balls.

SOUP

1. Bring the taro, pandan leaves, sugar, salt and water to the boil over a medium–high heat. Skim off any impurities and then simmer on a low heat for 5 minutes.

2. Add the sweet potato and coconut milk, return to the boil and skim off any impurities once again. Simmer on a low heat for 3 minutes.

3. Remove the pandan leaves.

Note: If you are not eating the *bubur cha cha* straight away, turn off the heat now and warm it up later just before serving. If using the homemade food colouring, add in the glutinous rice jellies as close to eating as possible, as the vibrant colours will start to fade (because they are natural extracts). If you are using artificial food colouring, feel free to add the jellies now.

4. Add the glutinous rice jellies and simmer. Once they rise to the surface, turn off the heat – the dessert is ready and can be cooled until needed.

5. This sweet soup can be served warm or chilled based on personal preference or the weather!

SERVES 6

HORLICKS PUDDING
AND PEANUT BRITTLE

SET PUDDING
525ml (2¼ cups) double (heavy) cream
2 tbsp cornflour (cornstarch), mixed with 2 tbsp water to form a slurry
60g (2¼oz) dark brown sugar
80g (2¾oz) Horlicks malt powder
¼ tsp salt

PEANUT BRITTLE
100g (3½oz) white sugar
100g (3½oz) peanuts, skinned and dry-toasted

This is another cracker from a collaboration with Guan.

The peanut brittle adds a welcome change of texture. If you're feeling lazy, this pudding also goes well with smashed-up, sweetened, dried banana chips.

I recommend that you start this recipe the day before to allow enough time for the pudding to set.

SET PUDDING
1. You'll need six pretty glasses or ramekins to set these in.
2. Put the double cream, sugar and Horlicks in a saucepan over a medium heat, stirring occasionally with a whisk to melt the sugar into the liquid. Do not boil.
3. When the cream comes to a gentle steam, whisk in the cornflour slurry.
4. Cook over a medium heat for 5 minutes, whisking and occasionally using a spatula to ensure the mixture isn't sticking to the edges of the pan. If it is thickening very quickly or is catching, turn down and/or take off the heat and whisk vigorously. When the pudding is ready it will look glossy and will thickly coat the back of a spoon.
5. Pour the pudding liquid into a measuring jug, then working quickly, pour it into the glasses. Allow to cool to room temperature before covering in cling film (plastic wrap). Leave to set in the fridge for at least 6 hours or preferably overnight.

PEANUT BRITTLE
1. Heat the sugar in a saucepan over a medium–low heat until it melts, stirring frequently with a spatula.
2. Once melted, tip in the peanuts and stir to coat. It may go grainy but keep going until the sugar melts again and they are all coated in the caramel.
3. Quickly pour out onto a baking-paper-lined baking sheet and spread it as flat as you can.
4. Allow to cool and then roughly smash into a loose rubble with a pestle and mortar.
5. To assemble the final puddings, put 1 tablespoon of peanut brittle on top of each pudding.

CHOCOLATE CARDAMOM CAKE

250ml (generous 1 cup) oil, plus extra for greasing

6 eggs

400g (14oz) white sugar

100g (3½oz) good-quality cocoa powder, dissolved in 250ml (generous 1 cup) hot water, and left to cool

300g (10½oz) ground almonds

1 tsp bicarbonate of soda (baking soda)

1 tsp ground cardamom

¼ tsp salt

200g (7oz) condensed milk

375g (13oz) Greek yoghurt

Dusting of icing (powdered) sugar (optional)

We served this dessert at our pop-up at Blend Café in Harringay in the autumn/winter of 2017. It was a runaway hit, especially with Jay Rayner when he came in: 'They have just one dessert, a soft and springy chocolate and cardamom cake served with a condiment which is a work of genius: condensed milk whipped up with Greek yogurt, the two ingredients soothing the harsher aspects of each other. If anybody out there already knew about this, why the hell didn't they tell me?'

This is essentially adapted from Nigella Lawson's chocolate olive oil cake which is also, very happily, gluten free!

1. Preheat the oven to 170°C/150°C fan/325°F/gas mark 3.

2. Line a 25 x 35cm (10 x 14in) baking sheet with baking paper and grease well with oil.

3. Beat the oil, eggs and sugar well with a hand blender until creamy, which will take around 3 minutes.

4. Turn the speed down and add in the cooled chocolate paste. Mix until blended, then add the ground almonds, bicarbonate of soda, cardamom and salt. Continue to combine until thoroughly incorporated.

5. Pour the mixture into the tin and bake in the middle of the oven for around 55–60 minutes, until a skewer poked into the middle comes out clean.

6. Cool the tin on a wire rack for 20 minutes, then tip the cake out onto a cutting board. Cut into 15 slices.

7. Mix the condensed milk with the Greek yoghurt.

8. Just before serving, cut each slice of cake into six pieces per portion so that each little square can be dipped into the condensed milk yoghurt. If you have it and are so inclined, dust a little icing sugar over the cake squares to make them look prettier.

SERVES 8

SWEET LONGAN TEA

40g (6 tbsp) dried lotus
  seeds
40g (7 tbsp) dried longan
  pulp
30g (5 tbsp) dried lily buds
1.8 litres (7¾ cups) water
120g (4¼oz) white sugar

I have strong memories of soothing *air mata kuching* from night-market hawker stalls. '*Air mata kuching*' literally translates to 'water and cat's eyes', as peeled, fresh longans can look like cat's eyes! This recipe replicates the Chinese version, *leng chee kang*, which has more chewy bits for texture.

This dish is deemed to have 'cooling' properties and may be served warm or cold with ice cubes. This explains its popularity in Malaysia, where the climate is hot and humid all year round. It is also popular around the Lunar New Year, where dried persimmons are usually added as they are in season.

This is perfect served chilled on a hot summer's evening, or warm on a wintry afternoon.

You'll need to start this recipe the day before simply to soak the lotus seeds overnight.

1. Soak the lotus seeds overnight in hot water. The next day, discard any black centres as they are bitter.
2. Rinse the dried longan and soak in 200ml (scant 1 cup) of hot water for 20 minutes. Drain the longan, reserving the soaking water and strain to remove any sediments. Rinse the longan in cold water.
3. Soak the lily bulbs in hot water for 30 minutes. Remove, rinse in cold water and drain.
4. Bring the water to the boil in a large saucepan.
5. Once it has come to the boil, add all of the ingredients, including the reserved longan soaking water, and simmer for 1 hour over the lowest heat until everything has softened.

MALAYSIA TRAVEL TIPS

I am often asked for recommendations for visiting Malaysia and so I've taken this opportunity to hardcode them as a bonus for you! You're welcome.

Please note that this section only reflects the places I personally know in Malaysia and is really just the tip of the iceberg. There are many other places that I haven't had the opportunity to visit or properly explore yet, like **Ipoh, Perlis, Johor Bahru, Kuching and Kota Kinabalu.** Just because a destination or specific eatery is not mentioned does not mean that it isn't worth a visit!

As a general note, it is not advisable to be outdoors between noon and 3 p.m. as it is *HOT.* It is usually well above 30°C (85°F) and very humid in Malaysia, which is why you will rarely see Malaysians walking for long distances. If we do, we will follow the shadows and/or use a nifty light-coloured umbrella with a reflective underside to protect us from the tremendous heat. So, during the hottest times of the day, seek refuge in your hotel or a mall. I highly recommend doing any sightseeing in the early morning or late afternoon. Malls are also a useful hideout for when it pours with rain, which it can do, suddenly and sharply!

We tend to move between air-conditioned spaces during the day, like malls or taxis. It is really useful to buy a local SIM card on arrival so that you can use your phone to order **Grab** taxis (Southeast Asia's Uber), as it can be awkward to get around, especially if you're heading to the suburbs. Try to save any such intrepid adventures for days with clearer weather as it is very difficult to get a taxi when it rains.

If staying in a hotel, buffets are generally of a high standard with a wide variety of Eastern and Western choices. We do like a hotel buffet for lunch or dinner as a special treat. You will often see large family groups doing this for celebratory meals, typically zoning in on the sushi bar and other seafood on offer. The beauty of hotel buffets is that they are in comfortable, air-conditioned surroundings. However, I would recommend not having breakfast at your hotel every day of your stay to save money and, more importantly, stomach space. Over the years I have learned that my eyes are always bigger than my stomach and now tend to have two main meals a day whenever I go back to Malaysia, with fresh-cut fruit or other small snacks whenever I am feeling peckish in between. Don't be afraid to just order one bowl of noodles between two at a hawker centre to be shared, to make the most of your eating capacity!

When visiting hawker centres or *kopi tiam* coffee shops, it is customary to order at least one drink between two from the person who comes round to offer them. It is considered rude not to. My favourite drink is freshly squeezed watermelon juice, closely followed by young coconut juice, sugar-cane juice, *limau ais* (sweetened calamansi lime juice), pearl barley stewed with a bit of syrup, cooling *cin cau* (herbal grass jelly), sweetened soybean milk or finally iced *teh tarik* (pulled tea) or *kopi* (coffee sweetened with condensed milk). If you prefer your tea or coffee black and unsweetened, just order *teh* or *kopi kosong* (kosong translates to 'empty', i.e. unsweetened).

Many hawker stalls will try upselling the 'special' version of their main dish. All this usually means is that the dish will come with additional meat or seafood. I have found it best to stick to the original version, as the ratio of meat/seafood to noodles is much better. English is commonly spoken in Malaysia. If all else fails, to order simply smile and point to what another customer is having!

Before your trip, please do double check the opening hours of any places I mention, as my information may be out of date. Note that most places will be closed at least one day a week and perhaps more during festive periods like Lunar New Year and Eid.

Massive thanks to my good friends Guan and Jo for introducing us to their favourite places around town. Do check out Guan's blog for more incredibly useful write-ups on KL, Penang and Kuching at:
www.theboywhoatetheworld.com/category/restaurant-reviews-2/kl-malaysia/

Thank you also to Lee Khang Yi, a food writer and journalist, and her partner Yuri for their consummate hospitality whenever we are in town.

KUALA LUMPUR

BREAKFAST

Most breakfast places start very early, sometimes from 6–11 a.m./noon. I will always go as early as possible when it is cooler.

In Malaysia, breakfast, lunch and dinner might include similar foods so there's less definition between meals (unlike say, in the West, where it might be common to eat more 'accepted' breakfast things in the morning like cereal). We adore eating savoury and/or spicy dishes like noodles, *roti canai* (flaky flatbreads) with curries and *nasi lemak* (coconut rice with sambal and other accoutrements) for breakfast but would very happily have any of these things for lunch or dinner, too.

For curry laksa, go to **Madras Lane, near Petaling Street** – choose the laksa stall in the middle, opposite the *yong tau fu* (tofu and vegetables stuffed with fish paste) stall which is also excellent.

Koon Kee Wan Tan Mee, also near **Petaling Street**, serves the most delicate dumplings with delicious QQ noodles. I love coming here with my mother, as she used to visit with her mother in her childhood. You can choose to order dry noodles (*kon lo wan tan mee*) or in soup (*wan tan tong mee*). Juicy *char siu* (Chinese barbecue pork), tender poached chicken or roast duck can also be added. There is also a branch in **Petaling Jaya**.

Also near **Petaling Street**, at the end of **Jalan Hang Lekir** where it crosses with **Jalan Sultan**, there is an Indian drinks stall selling fabulous *cendol* (strands of fragrant pandan jelly with shaved ice, palm sugar and salted coconut milk).

Village Park Nasi Lemak is well worth a taxi ride out to the suburbs for its fluffy coconut rice and phenomenal fried chicken.

MUST EAT: **ICC Pudu Market** for toast slathered in *kaya* (coconut jam) with half-cooked eggs eaten with soy sauce and white pepper at **Ah Weng Koh Hainan Tea** — the classic Malaysian breakfast. Also get the *pohpia* (fresh spring rolls) from the nearby hawker stall. The stalls closer to the entrance are better. Laksa is also available here!

Goon Wah Restaurant, Kuchai Lama for DIY *loh shee fun* (delicate slippery noodles served in a blistering hot claypot with deep-fried lard and savoury goodness). The fish-head noodle soup is super-comforting here. It has an air-conditioned section and is also open for lunch when it is full of local office workers. There is also a branch in **Petaling Jaya**.

If staying in SS2, I love **Loong Seng** dim sum for its massive, old-school steamers. They will bring out trays of different dishes for you to choose from. I often dream of their congee which is full of finely chopped dried oysters, century egg and tofu skin.

Feeka Coffee Roasters near **Jalan Alor** is a nice coffee shop in which to chill with free wi-fi.

Visit **Chow Kit**, the largest wet produce market in KL, situated along **Jalan Tuanku Abdul Rahman**, between the hours of 9 a.m. and 5 p.m. daily.

LUNCH/ALL-DAY DINING

I would urge you to seek out the curry-puff stall in **Brickfields**, which sells the best spiral curry puffs and fried battered bananas known to man. It is only open until the mid-afternoon and usually has a massive queue.

The egg tarts at **Bunn Choon**, near **Petaling Street**, are among the best I've ever tasted — the charcoal pastry is extra crisp.

There are many good stalls in the **Lot 10 mall** basement food court, as the aim was to bring

together the best hawkers of KL into one central location. The claypot noodles are great as is the Penang duck egg *char kway teow*. Order the *ais kacang*, also known as ABC, an acronym of *air batu campur* (shaved ice with red beans, sweetcorn, rose syrup and other textural delights) from the dessert/drinks stall. When ordering, ask for less ice for a better flavour-to-ice ratio in the *ais kacang*.

If you want an adventure, head to **Sambal Hijau** for incredible Malay/Indonesian *nasi campur*. It's worth the trip for a pick-and-mix choice of over 80 dishes with rice!

Baba Low's, Bangsar sells excellent *cendol* and Peranakan food.

Ganga Cafe, Bangsar has incredible south Indian vegetarian food, including *vadai* (savoury doughnuts), all sorts of *roti* and biryani. Its Sunday buffet brunch is especially good value but you won't get the same variety as ordering à la carte.

If you are in need of air-con at lunch, **Madam Kwan's**, **The Chicken Rice Shop** and **Nyonya Colours** are good chain restaurants serving a reliably decent range of dishes. You'll find branches in most malls. All malls will also have a budget food court where the basic standard is good.

KLCC Suria Mall is worth a look, especially Kinokuniya bookshop if hunting down cookbooks only available in Asia. Mid Valley Megamall is another of my favourites.

KL International Airport also has a budget food court called the Food Garden on Level 2.

I have a big soft spot for **KFC** in Malaysia, especially during festive seasons. Generally, order the zinger chicken (unavailable in other parts of the world) for pieces of chicken in a delicious crunchy, spicy batter, with mash and gravy. One of the best things I had on one trip was their Chinese New Year salted egg and curry-leaf fried chicken special. Incredibly good!

DINNER

MUST EAT: **Roti Valentine**. Order the *roti ½ telur* (flaky flatbreads roughly chopped, then covered with super-tasty dhal, a half-cooked egg and a generous dollop of sambal), crispy *roti garing* (extra thin and crispy flatbreads) and paper-thin *roti tisu* (very thin flatbread rolled into a tall cone) drizzled with condensed milk. There's no air-con, so go after 7 p.m. if possible.

Try the banana-leaf rice at **Vishals, Brickfields**. No air-con, so go after 7 p.m. if possible.

Heun Kee Claypot Chicken Rice, Pudu, serves very tasty claypot rice with chicken, Chinese *lap cheong* sausage and salted fish, cooked over hellishly hot charcoal flames. Leave it to rest for as long as possible when it reaches your table so that it develops a nice crust on the bottom. Order the tofu stuffed with seafood as a side dish. Air-con available.

MUST EAT: Visit **Meng Kee restaurant**, about halfway down **Jalan Alor**, for *kam heong* golden, fragrant clams and stir-fried butter prawns – order the latter without shells. Only order a dish for two people maximum at any of the seafood restaurants on Jalan Alor, as the portions are generous! The chicken wings from **Wong Ah Wah**, at the end of **Jalan Alor**, are great, as is the satay stall next door.

SS2 hawker centre, **Petaling Jaya** – the hawker centre of my childhood against which all others are measured.

Go to **Restoran Millennium Eighty Six in Paramount Gardens**, **Petaling Jaya** for *wat tan hor* (flat rice noodles in silky-smooth egg gravy), KL stir-fried *hokkien mee* with crispy fried lard, fiercely bubbling claypot Chinese-style fishhead curry, *lobak* (tofu-skin spring rolls), *otak otak* (fish with spiced custard in banana leaf) and satay. A classic example of a *kopi tiam* coffee shop.

PENANG

Thank you so much to Nazia and Joel for being our chauffeurs and guides on our 2018 visit.

I would definitely include a few days (at least three nights if it's your first visit) up in Penang on any trip to Malaysia, as it is one of our renowned food capitals. I would recommend staying within **Georgetown** itself for convenience.

Penang Peranakan Museum and the **Cheong Fatt Tze Blue Mansion** are must-visits as they are beautiful.

MUST EAT: Go to **Cecil Street Market**, a bustling hawker centre, for breakfast and lunch. Find the amazing white curry mee stall and go nuts buying a variety of *kuih* (Malaysian cakes and snacks) and prawn fritters.

Have a wander around **Pulau Tikus** wet produce market in the morning.

Try **Sri Weld** hawker centre for **Ali Nasi Lemak**, an excellent breakfast.

MUST EAT: **Old Siam Road Char Kway Teow** or **Ah Leng Char Kway Teow**.

MUST EAT: Visit **888 Hokkien Mee** for the best prawn noodle soup! Add on the *siew yuk* (crispy pork belly) and get a fantastic *ais kacang* to cool yourself down from the stall manned by a friendly uncle just in front.

MUST EAT: **Restaurant Taman Emas** opposite the girls' school serves the best assam laksa on the island, in my opinion. Perfect, crunchy little spring rolls are an automatic side order here, as is fresh nutmeg juice.

Visit **Penang Road Teochew Cendol** for the famous stall with the long queue.

Good dinner hawker-centre options are **Chulia Street Night Market** in **Chinatown** and also **New Lane** near **Komtar**. You will be spoiled for choice!

Line Clear Nasi Kandar (24 hours) and **Deen Maju Nasi Kandar** (lunch and dinner) are great options for Mamak Indian *nasi campur*.

Go to **Kebaya** at the **Seven Terraces Hotel** for great Peranakan food with stunning decor. Air conditioned.

Perut Rumah Nyonya Restaurant is a must for homely Peranakan food. Air conditioned.

Visit **Pasar Air Itam** for the most famous assam laksa on the island, and you should also order the *lobak* while you're here. You can visit the **Kek Lok Si Temple** and/or take the cable car up **Penang Hill** to add value to your journey.

MUST EAT: For the intrepid, take a 20-minute taxi ride out of Georgetown to **Nasi Melayu Lidiana** in **Tanjung Bunga** for absolutely cracking Malay *nasi campur*.

MELAKA/MALACCA

Make sure to visit on a Friday or Saturday, and include an overnight stay so that you can spend an evening exploring the weekend night market on **Jonker Street**.

Baba Charlie Cafe is great for the full gamut of Peranakan dishes and *kuih*.

Try **Kocik Kitchen** for great *kuih pie tee* (crispy pastry shells filled with braised vegetables), stir-fried four-angled beans, *otak otak* and *cendol*.

Putu Piring Melaka, **Jalan Tengkara** is the place to go for one of my favourite Malaysian sweet snacks, a delicate steamed rice flour cake filled with unctuous just-melted *gula melaka* (caramelized palm sugar). Heaven.

BEACH-RESORT ISLANDS

I would recommend **Pangkor Laut** as it is an exclusive resort with chalets built over the crystal-clear sea. Full-on luxury. Otherwise, visit the **Perhentian Islands** or **Redang**, if snorkelling is your thing. If visiting **Langkawi**, rent a car so you can follow the night market around the island for dinner!

ACKNOWLEDGEMENTS

MOST THANKS TO MY FAMILY FOR YOUR LOVE AND UNWAVERING SUPPORT:

My mum Maxine who teaches me how to cook even to this day, and for always feeding me when I need it most;

My dad Gregory for being my bookkeeper, handyman and emergency stock runner. I am pleased that you cannot fault my assam laksa!;

My brother Geoffrey for being a regular customer and for that one time helping me man the street-food stall on a cold, wintry evening in Brixton;

Owen for being my sounding board, best friend, confidant, marketing adviser, all-round rock;

My cousin Hannah for the free branding work at the start of my journey and volunteering at the stall when I was in need;

My cousin May Lee for being a staunch advocate of my sauces from the beginning; and Audrey Bain and the Edinburgh/New Zealand family for being my perennial cheerleaders.

You are only ever as strong as the people you surround yourself with. Thank you to all my staff, past and present. My greatest joy running the business is the familial bond I share with you. Thank you for having my back. Without you, I have nothing.

To my oldest friends from school, university and the law, thank you for continually celebrating my successes and shouting about them far and wide. Julia Foye, Tashvin Ramdarshan, Richard Wong, Thash Pillay, Anita Panesar, Laura Titcombe, Sarah Ellis, Elina Man, Lucy Hall and Theresa Hickman. To Seth Peterson whom I lost to cancer in April 2020, I miss you. Thank you Brídin Allen for pushing me to take the first step by opening social media accounts for the business back in 2013!

Thank you to every single customer who

Credit: Charlotte Hu

has supported me over the years. Special thanks go to my regulars. Your friendship and encouragement means the world to me: Anna Sulan Masing, @ClerkenwellboyEC1, Kar-Shing Tong, Chris and Natasha Keeling, Matt Stavrou, Georgia Scrghiou, Emma Hughes, Hui Ting Heng, Perm Paitayawat, Ed Smith, Chris Prowler, Bernard Ho and family, Izzy Raja Ariff and family, Emily and Amy Chung, Rida Bilgrami, Angela Sam, Han Wei Teo and Serena Mariani, Steve Talevski, Linda Zubairi, Pascal Barker, Nazia du Bois, Ed and Geoff Tan, Steve Cooper, Vanessa Toh, Joy Hinson, Jack Tan, Hannah Peterkin, Raj Popat, Tze How Mok, Jacqui Murrell, Keefy Yap, Corinne Rowe, Dan Calladine, Catherine and Gavin Hanly, Marissa Mahendra, Melissa Thompson, Martha de Lacey, Felicity Cloake, Lizzie Mabbott, Lizzy Barber and Lara Bulut.

Wilkes McDermid, credit: Bridin Allen

TO ALL THE JOURNALISTS WHO HAVE EVER GIVEN ME A PLATFORM, ESPECIALLY:

Jay Rayner for first putting us on the map in 2016;

Grace Dent for believing in me – your review of our newly opened restaurant in 2018 really cemented everything, thank you;

The Eater London crew: Jonathan Nunn, Angela Hui, George Reynolds, Adam Coghlan, James Hansen, David Jay Paw; and

Allan Jenkins, Molly Tait-Hyland at the *Observer Food Monthly*.

WILKES McDERMID:

Wilkes was a food blogger and a key proponent of the fledgling street-food scene in London in 2010–2015. He was an avid, loyal supporter of all of us street-food traders at the time, like

Bleecker Burger, Bao, Donostia Social Club, Breddos Tacos and Pizza Pilgrims. If we were at a new market or at an event, he would be the first in line to show his support and to take amazing photographs of us and the food. Wilkes made it his purpose to record the people and stories behind street food.

I only knew Wilkes for just over a year before he took his own life in February 2015 after years of suffering from depression. In just a few months, he introduced me to everyone he knew and was one of my strongest advocates. He fought for me to be given my first market pitch in Harringay.

This first restaurant is, in part, for him. He was also Malaysian and loved laksa. I think he would have liked mine. I owe you, Wilkes, and I'm looking forward to sharing a negroni with you again one day.

INDUSTRY ALLIES:

I owe a great deal to many industry peers: Colin Tu of Salvation in Noodles, Guan Leong Chua, Lap-fai Lee, Zeren Wilson, Matt Chatfield, Tim Mawn, Asma Khan of Darjeeling Express,

Credit: Lap-fai Lee

Credit: Bridin Allen

Lee Tiernan of Black Axe Mangal, Saima Khan of The Hampstead Kitchen, Alexis Noble of Wander, Vanessa Goh and the Rice Guys/Pezu team, Sabrina Ghayour, Ping Coombes, John and Yee Li of Dumplingshack, Yotam Ottolenghi, Helen Goh, Karan Gokani of Hoppers, Elizabeth Haigh of Mei Mei, Tong Tong Ren and Pei Ran Gong of Chinese Laundry, John Torode, Emma Reynolds of Tonkotsu, Sirichai Kularbwong of Singburi, Ben Chapman of Kiln, Chantelle Nicholson of Tredwells, Crispin Somerville of the Quo Vadis group, Calum Franklin of Holborn Dining Room, Nud Dudhia and Chris Whitney of Breddos Tacos. Thank you for your advice, friendship, and crushingly generous hospitality.

Over the years I have had the privilege to host events and collaborate with several of the above. I have used these as an opportunity to connect, to share ideas and to learn new skills and be inspired. Running a restaurant can be lonely and isolating at times, so it is comforting to know that so many others are in the same boat, and have the same worries and stresses in their businesses, too. It is, of course, always a joy to work with people I love, respect, and admire. I look forward to many more to come.

Special shout out to Ben Kulchstein of Dalston Chillies for allowing me to continually pick your brains about pesky sauce jarring!

Finally, thank you to my book team! Nicola Chang for securing my book deal. Céline Hughes and Claire Rochford of Quadrille. Nicole Herft, Louise Hagger, Alexander Breeze, Simone Shagam and Sophie Bronze for making my vision come to life in this book. Tamsin English for finessing my words. A massive shout out to Alex Green, my designer – it is his branding work that has really helped to shape the restaurant's identity from the beginning.

I would not be where I am today without everyone mentioned in these pages.

Thank you ☺

Credit: ClerkenwellboyEC1

Credit: David Jay Paw

INDEX

PUBLISHING DIRECTOR: Sarah Lavelle
SENIOR COMMISSIONING EDITOR: Céline Hughes
EDITORIAL ASSISTANT: Sofie Shearman
HEAD OF DESIGN: Claire Rochford
ART DIRECTION AND DESIGN: Alexander Green
PHOTOGRAPHER: Louise Hagger
PHOTOGRAPHER'S ASSISTANT: Sophie Bronze
FOOD STYLIST: Nicole Herft
FOOD STYLIST'S ASSISTANT: Simone Shagam
PROP STYLIST: Alexander Breeze
HEAD OF PRODUCTION: Stephen Lang
PRODUCTION CONTROLLER: Sabeena Atchia

First published in 2021 by Quadrille,
an imprint of Hardie Grant Publishing

Reprinted in 2022, 2024
10 9 8 7 6 5 4 3

QUADRILLE
52–54 Southwark Street
London SE1 1UN
quadrille.com

Cataloguing in Publication Data: a catalogue record
for this book is available from the British Library.

Text © Mandy Yin 2021
Photography © Louise Hagger 2021 (except pages
4, 10–11, 13, 15–16, 29–31, 45, 69, 73, 80–81,
157, 235–249 © Mandy Yin 2021 or as credited)
Design and layouts © Quadrille 2021

ISBN 978 1 78713 704 2

Printed in China